TEACH Y

SPANISH
VOCABULARY
A COMPLETE LEARNING TOOL

SPANISH VOCABULARY

A COMPLETE LEARNING TOOL

Series Editor: Rosi McNab

Language Editor: Pilar Caldeiro López

TEACH YOURSELF BOOKS

For UK orders: please contact Bookpoint Ltd, 130 Milton Park, Abingdon, Oxon OX14 4SB. Telephone: (44) 01235 827720, Fax: (44) 01235 400454. Lines are open from 09.00–18.00, Monday to Saturday, with a 24-hour message answering service. You can also order through our website www.madaboutbooks.com

For U.S.A. order enquiries: please contact McGraw-Hill Customer Services, P.O. Box 545, Blacklick, OH 43004-0545, U.S.A. Telephone 1-800-722-4726. Fax: 1-614-755-5645.

For Canada order enquiries: please contact McGraw-Hill Ryerson Ltd., 300 Water St, Whitby, Ontario L1N 9B6, Canada. Telephone: 905 430 5000. Fax: 905 430 5020.

Long renowned as the authoritative source for self-guided learning – with more than 30 million copies sold worldwide – the *Teach Yourself* series includes over 300 titles in the fields of languages, crafts, hobbies, business and education.

British Library Cataloguing in Publication Data
A catalogue record for this title is available from The British Library

Library of Congress Catalog Card Number: 95–71314

First published in UK 1996 by Hodder Headline Plc, 338 Euston Road, London NW1 3BH.

First published in US 1996 by Contemporary Books, A Division of The McGraw-Hill Companies, 1 Prudential Plaza, 130 East Randolph Street, Chicago, Illinois 60601 U.S.A.

The 'Teach Yourself' name and logo are registered trade marks of Hodder & Stoughton Ltd.

Typeset by Transet Limited, Coventry, England.
Printed in Great Britain for Hodder & Stoughton Educational, a division of Hodder Headline Ltd, 338 Euston Road, London NW1 3BH by Cox & Wyman Ltd, Reading, Berkshire.

Impression number	18	17	16	15	14	13	12	11
Year		2007	2006	2005	2004	2003	2002	

CONTENTS

INTRODUCTION

─────── About this book ───────

This book is an easy-to-use reference book of key language for the language student, business traveller and holidaymaker.

It is designed to be EASY to use, both:
- as a quick reference to find useful words in a specific area, and
- to increase your word power by building up a stock of new vocabulary.

─────── How to use the book ───────

The words in each topic are divided into further sub-topics for easy reference, for example within the major topic area of *La casa, el hogar y el jardín* (House, home and garden), you will find amongst other sub-topics *Las partes de la casa* (Parts of the house). Within these sub-topics, the words are further divided into smaller groupings with other words of similar meaning. There are also some examples of how words might be used in a sentence.

─── Pronunciation of Spanish: ───
guidelines

Spanish pronunciation is relatively easy to learn as there are fewer different sounds than in English and in general spelling and pronunciation go together. The following guidelines are of course no substitute for first hand exposure to the language, so students should take every opportunity to listen to native speakers and to imitate what they hear.

Introduction

The Spanish alphabet

The Spanish alphabet now has 27 letters, of which 26 are common to English and Spanish. The extra letter is **ñ**.

The Spanish alphabet is therefore:

a	j	r
b	k	s
c	l	t
d	m	u
e	n	v
f	ñ	w
g	o	x
h	p	y
i	q	z

You may find that other books and dictionaries say there are 30 letters in the Spanish alphabet. This is because there are three sounds particular to Spanish: **ch**, **ll**, **rr**. Until recently, all of these were considered as separate letters, although in 1994 it was officially decided that they will no longer be considered as such.

Spanish vowels

Spanish vowels are very pure sounds, and each has only one pronunciation. They are pronounced in a clear, somewhat sharp way and English speakers need to make an effort to give each vowel its own, particular pronunciation, and to avoid the temptation of giving them the unstressed vowel sound which is so common in English (as in words such as not**a**ble, penc**i**l, Lond**o**n).

a   slightly longer than the 'a' of 'cat'
       mañana; **Salamanca**; **para**
       Note that in the first example, the three **a**'s all have the same "clear" pronunciation. Do not pronounce the second **a** 'ar', as in 'car'.

e   similar to the 'e' in 'get'
       Enrique; **Benavente**; **empresa**

Introduction

i   like the 'ee' in 'seen'
     fino; rico
     a 'y' at the end of the word is pronounced in the same way:
     rey; ley
o   if the syllable ends in 'o' it is pronounced like the 'o' in 'vote'
     poco; bravo; esto
     if the syllable ends in a consonant, it has a shorter
     pronunciation, like the 'o' in 'off'
     sol; costa
u   like the 'oo' in 'pool'
     luna; museo; música
     Note however that the **u** is silent after **q** and between **g** and **e**
     or **i**:
     Guernica; Miguel; guitarra; guía
     unless there are two dots over it:
     pingüino; Sigüenza

Diphthongs

When a 'strong' vowel (**a**, **o** or **e**) combines with a 'weak' vowel (**i** or **u**)
it is known as a diphthong.

ai/ay   like 'i' in 'hide'
         baile; hay
au   like 'ou' in 'found'
         causa; bautizo
ei/ey   like 'ay' in 'pay'
         reina; ley
ie   like 'ye' in 'yellow'
         viejo; cien
oi/oy   like 'oy' in 'toy'
         oiga; voy

Spanish Consonants

b, v   have the same sound, similar to an English 'b' but a little
        softer. The English sound 'v' does not exist in Spanish.
        vino; bar; abanico

3

c	like 'th' in 'thick' when followed by **e** or **i**

c like 'th' in 'thick' when followed by **e** or **i**
Barcelona; Valencia; hacer; cerveza
like 'c' in 'car' when followed by **a, o, u** or a consonant
cantar; comer; crimen

ch like the 'ch' in 'child'
mucho; leche; churro

d between vowels and after consonants (except **l** and **n**) the 'd' has a very soft pronunciation, like 'th' in 'the'
cada; sidra
at the end of words it has an even softer pronunciation, and is often omitted
usted; ciudad; Madrid
otherwise, it is pronounced like the 'd' in 'date'
día; delante; andar

f like 'f' in 'four'
café; foto

g has two pronunciations:
– guttural, like **j**, when it is followed by an **e** or **i**
gitano; general
– as in the English 'gut' when it is followed by **a, o** or **u**
gato; agosto; agua

h is always silent in Spanish
hotel; hielo; Alhambra

j has a guttural sound, rather like the Scottish 'ch' in 'loch'
jamón; Rioja; naranja

k is rare in Spanish. Pronounced like 'k' in 'king'
kilo; Kodak

l like 'l' in 'like'
Inglaterra, español

ll like the 'lli' in 'million'
Sevilla; paella; millón

m like 'm' in 'milk'
mucho; mano

n like 'n' in 'not'
pan; nada

ñ This is different to a normal **n**, and is pronounced like the 'ni' in 'onion'.
señor; señorita; España
There are no common words which begin with **ñ**.

Introduction

p   like 'p' in 'pull' but without an aspiration
       guapo; padre; pescado
q   is always pronounced like 'k' in 'king' and never like the 'qu' in
       'queen'
       quiosco; queso
r   is always "rolled" - with one or two flips of the tip of the tongue
       sombrero; señorita
       At the beginning of a word **r** is pronounced like **rr**.
rr   has an even more noticeable roll than **r**
       ferrocarril; carretera
s   like 's' in 'some'
       casa; sangre; secreto
       except before a 'voiced consonant' (**b, d, g, l, m** and **n**) when it
       is like the 's' in 'hose'
       desde; mismo
t   like 't' in 'tennis' but without an aspiration
       también; taza; patata
v   see the note on 'b'
w   is really only found in English words which have been
       absorbed into the Spanish language. It is pronounced like a **b/v**
       wáter (*lavatory*); **waterpolo**;
       or kept as an English 'w'
       Walkman™; whisky
x   before a vowel, usually like 'ex' in 'excellent' (not 'example')
       máximo
       before a consonant, usually like 's' in 'sad'
       extra; sexto
z   like 'th' in 'thing'
       zapato; zumo; andaluz

Stress Rules

Spanish words are stressed on the last syllable if they end in a
consonant other than **n** or **s**:
español; hablar
They are stressed on the last but one syllable if they end in **n** or **s** or a
vowel:
billete; gasolina; comprenden; muchachas
The majority of Spanish words fall into this category.

Introduction

If a word breaks either of these rules, an accent is written to show where the stress falls:

sábado; **teléfono**; **habitación**

All words ending in **-ión** carry the stress in this way.

So if you see a word with a written accent, you must stress the syllable where the accent is placed. (Failure to do this could result in a misunderstanding.)

An accent is also used to differentiate between words of identical spelling but with different meanings:

si (*if*), **sí** (*yes*); **el** (*the*), **él** (*he*)

Pronunciation practice

Now practise your pronunciation by saying:

1 All the words you can remember from the examples;
2 Then try these:
   La paella es un plato típico de Valencia.
   Dos botellas de vino de Rioja
   Un zumo de naranja
   El rey de España se llama Juan Carlos.
   Un vaso de agua con hielo
   Un billete de ida y vuelta
   ¡Lleno, por favor!
   Sí, hablo español.
   En Madrid, quiero comprar una guitarra y un abanico.
   Una guía de hoteles españoles

Vocabulary learning

Follow the simple suggestions in this introduction to help you to increase your vocabulary.

There are also *¡Otra vez!* (Once again!) activities with which to test yourself and so make learning easier.

So how can I learn more effectively?

Most people complain of having a poor memory. They say they are no good at learning a language because they can't remember the words, but few people have difficulty in remembering things which really interest them: the names of members of a football team, the parts of a car, what happened in the last episode of a favourite radio or TV series, the ingredients in a recipe ...!

How can I make learning a list of words more interesting?

1 First YOU decide which list you are going to learn today.
2 Then YOU decide which words in that list you want to try to learn.
   Mark each word. (Put a mark beside each word you have chosen.)
   Count them. (How many are you going to try to learn?)
   Underline the first letter of each word. (What letters do they begin with?)
   Now you are ready to begin.
3 Say the words ALOUD. If you put your hands over your ears whilst you read them it will cut out extraneous noise and help you to concentrate by reflecting the sound of your voice and helping you to hear what you sound like. You should have studied the previous section in this introduction on pronunciation before doing this.
4 Next look for ways to learn them. Do you know how YOU learn words best?

Learning

Try this quick test to find out how you learn best:

• Look at the words with translations in *Method 1*, and the illustrated word list in *Method 2* for one minute and try to remember as many words as possible.
• Close the book and write down in Spanish a list of the words you remember.

Introduction

Method 1: translated lists

el caballo	*horse*	el zapato	*shoe*
la botella	*bottle*	el plátano	*banana*
el cuchillo	*knife*	el avión	*aeroplane*
el pan	*bread*	la puerta	*gate*
la bufanda	*scarf*	el libro	*book*
la carta	*letter*	la taza	*cup*

Method 2: illustrations

el árbol   la bicicleta   la bombilla   el elefante   la flor   los guantes

el grifo   la manzana   el reloj   la silla   la ventana   el barco

Have you remembered more words from the the group of illustrated words, or or from the word list?

If you have remembered more of the words from the list rather than from the pictures, you have a preference for memorising the written word and you may find it helpful to write down the words you are learning.

If you have remembered more of the illustrated words, this shows you have a more visual memory. You will probably find it helpful to 'tie in' the words you learn to a quick drawing.

If you didn't remember many at all, try again using these different techniques:

Method 3: composite pictures

Imagining a composite picture can help you remember the words. Imagine a boat (*un barco*), 'put' an elephant (*un elefante*), eating an apple (*una manzana*), sitting on a chair (*una silla*) in the boat. 'Put' a tap (*un grifo*) on the front of the boat to let the water out. (5 words).

Introduction

Look through a window (*una ventana*) at a Christmas tree (*un árbol de Navidad*), 'hang' a bicycle (*una bicicleta*), a flower (*una flor*) and a clock (*un reloj*) in the tree like Christmas decorations. Now put a light bulb (*una bombilla*) on the top. (6 words) What have you got left? Some gloves (*unos guantes*) – put them on to keep your hands warm.

Method 4: first letter groups

Grouping words by their first letter and first few letters can help you remember the words. Look again at the words in Method 1.
There are three which begin with **c: cab...; car...; cuch...**
There are three which begin with **p: p...; pl...;pu...**(you can eat two of them)
There are two which begin with **b: bo...; bu...**
There is one of each which begin with **a...; l...; t...; z...**
Now how many can you remember?

Which methods are best for me?

By which of these four methods do you remember best? Just one? Or a mixture of all of them?

Try again in five minutes ... and in half an hour ... and tomorrow.

Now you should know how you prefer to learn!

Learning AND remembering

It's one thing to remember words a short time after you have learned them. But will you remember them when you come across them again in the future? Stages **1-4** below revise the inital learning part of the process already described previously; stages **5** and beyond help you find 'pegs' in your mind on which to 'hang' the words you have learned, and so remember them better.

1 Below is a list of twelve words. Choose six of them to learn.

el aparcamiento	*car park*	la parada de autobús	*bus stop*
la autopista	*motorway*	el paso a nivel	*level crossing*
la carretera	*road*	el puente	*bridge*
el cruce	*crossroads*	el semáforo	*traffic lights*
la esquina	*corner*	la señal	*sign*
la estación	*station*	la zona peatonal	*pedestrian area*

Introduction

2 Put a **mark** beside the words you would like to learn.
Count them. (Choose six to try).
Underline the first letter of each word.

3 Read them aloud. (Put your hands over your ears whilst you do it). Try it again, until you are happy with the sound of them.

4 Now learn the words using the method or combination of methods (described previously) which suits you best.

5 Look at each word carefully for ways to remember it. Find 'pegs' to hang them on.

Does it sound like the English word*? (**estación** – *station*)
Does it sound like a different English word*? (**esquina** – sounds like *skin*)
Does part of it look like the English word*? (a{**parc**}amiento – *car park*)
* see the next section: *Tips for remembering*
Can you find any word that might be helpful? (**auto** – to do with cars)
Can you see a picture of each word, as you say it?
Can you picture it as it sounds? (**cruce** – *crossroads*)
Can you build all the words into an imaginary composite picture?
Say each word as you 'add' it to the picture.
(**carretera**; **cruce**; **semáforo**; ...)

6 Cover up the English and try to remember what your chosen words mean.

7 Write a list of the first letters and put dashes for the missing letters.
Which did you choose? **Mark** them ... and try to 'read' the words.

el a _ _ _ _ _ _ _ _ _ _ _	*car park* (parc/park)
la a _ _ _ _ _ _ _ _	*motorway* (auto)
la c _ _ _ _ _ _ _ _	*road* (car)
el c _ _ _ _	*crossroads* (first two letters same as English)
la e _ _ _ _ _ _	*corner* (sounds like skin)
la e _ _ _ _ _ _ _	*station* (sounds like the English word)
la p _ _ _ _ _ _ _ _ _ _ _ _ _	*bus stop* (bus)
el p _ _ _ _ _ _ _ _ _	*level crossing* (**nivel** sounds like level)
el p _ _ _ _ _	*bridge* (imagine punt going under bridge)

10

el s _ _ _ _ _ _ _	*traffic lights* (semaphore signals)
la s _ _ _ _	*sign* (sounds fairly similar)
la z _ _ _ _ _ _ _ _ _ _ _	*pedestrian area* (zone/area)

8 Fill in the missing letters and check that you have got them right.

9 Cover up the Spanish and see if you can remember the words you have chosen.

10 Do something else for half an hour.

11 Go back and check that you can still remember the six you chose.

car park	**el a** _ _ _ _ _ _ _ _ _ _ _ _
motorway	**la a** _ _ _ _ _ _ _ _
road	**la c** _ _ _ _ _ _ _ _
crossroads	**el c** _ _ _ _
corner	**la e** _ _ _ _ _ _
station	**la e** _ _ _ _ _ _ _
bus stop	**la p** _ _ _ _ _ _ _ _ _ _ _ _ _ _
level crossing	**el p** _ _ _ _ _ _ _ _ _
bridge	**el p** _ _ _ _ _
traffic lights	**el s** _ _ _ _ _ _ _
sign	**la s** _ _ _ _
pedestrian area	**la z** _ _ _ _ _ _ _ _ _ _ _

Tips for remembering

A good short cut to remembering is by linking Spanish to what you already know of English and/or other languages.

Words related to English

Does it sound like the English word or a related word?
The Spanish word for square is **plaza** – it sounds a bit like *place*
Does it look like the English word or a related word?
The Spanish word for garden is **jardín** – virtually the same word
The Spanish word for vegetable garden is **huerta** – as in *horticulture*

English is a particularly rich language with words from many sources. Some of the words we use come from a Northern origin, from

Introduction

the ancient Anglo-Saxon and Nordic languages and some from a Southern origin, from Latin, French and the Celtic languages as well as many words brought back by the early travellers from all round the globe.

Some examples of words used in English whose origin is in the Spanish language are:

chocolate	**chocolate**
potato	**patata**
guitar	**guitarra**
hammock	**hamaca**
cannibal	**canibal**
hurricane	**huracán**

English and Spanish share many words of Latin origin, which often makes learning new vocabulary easy. A few examples of words which are virtually the same (apart from pronunciation) are:

admiración	*admiration*
beneficio	*benefit*
calcular	*calculate*
dedicado	*dedicated*
formación	*formation*

Look for words that are similar to the English ones e.g. **Diario** is the Spanish word for 'newspaper'. It sounds like the English word 'diary'. **Día** means 'day' in Spanish, so **diario** really means 'daily'.

Repeated patterns between English and Spanish

Consonant/vowel changes

The English 'ph' is always **'f'** in Spanish

telephone	**teléfono**
photo	**foto**
graphic	**gráfico**

'-ed' at the end of an English word is often **'-ado'** or **'-ido'** in Spanish

reserved	**reservado**
included	**incluido**

Introduction

'-tion' at the end of an English word becomes **'-ción'** in Spanish
>*administration* **administración**
>*relation* **relación**

'ss' in English is often **'s'** in Spanish
>*permissive* **permisivo**
>*possessive* **posesivo**

'imm' in English becomes **'inm'** in Spanish
>*immediate* **inmediato**
>*immense* **inmenso**

'b' in English often changes to **'v'** in Spanish, and vice versa
>*automobile* **automóvil**
>*have* **haber**

's' at the beginning of a word becomes **'es'** in Spanish
>*school* **escuela**
>*state* **estado**

'th' at the beginning of a word in English is often just **'t'** in Spanish
>*theatre* **teatro**
>*thermometer* **termómetro**

English compound nouns

One characteristic of English is that two nouns can go together to form a compound noun, for example 'bread knife', 'shoulder bag', 'window frame' etc. In Spanish, the most common way of expressing these ideas is by reversing the nouns and adding **'de'** between them: 'credit card' therefore becomes **'tarjeta de crédito'** (literally 'card of credit'). Other examples are:

el billete de avión *plane ticket*
el número de asiento *seat number*
la tarjeta de embarque *boarding card*
la salida de emergencia *emergency exit*

Spanish adjectives as nouns

In Spanish, adjectives can also be used as nouns, whereas this is very rare in English. For example, 'the white ones' would be **'los blancos/las blancas'**; 'the red one' would be **'el rojo/la roja'**.

Introduction

Words related to other European languages

Look for words that are related to words you already know. A brief look at some of the other European languages may help you to recognise patterns that will help you to deduce the meaning of new words and help you to learn them more quickly.

English	German	French	Italian	Spanish	related English
father	Vater	père	padre	padre	paternity
flower	Blumen	fleur	flora	flor	bloom; floral
foot	Fuß	pied	piede	pie	pedal
grass	Gras	herbe	herba	hierba	herb
hunger	Hunger	faim	fame	hambre	famished
iron	Eisen	fer	ferro	hierro	ferrous (Fe)
man	Mann	homme	huomo	hombre	human
meat	Fleisch	viande	carne	carne	carnivorous; flesh
water	Wasser	eau	aqua	agua	aquarium

The English words in the column below are all of a 'Northern' origin, but each has related words from a 'Southern' origin which in many cases are very similar to the Spanish words. See if you can find the related words from the following list and add them to the right-hand column:

cavalry; chamber; corporation; corpse; dentist; habit; lunar; marine; mermaid; mural; nocturnal; robe; vest; terrestrial

English	French	Italian	Spanish	related English words
body	corps	corpo	cuerpo	
dress	robe	abito	vestido	
earth	terre	terra	tierra	
horse	cheval	cavallo	caballo	
moon	lune	luna	luna	
night	nuit	notte	noche	
room	chambre	camera	cámara	
sea	mer	mare	mar	
tooth	dent	dente	diente	
wall	mur	muro	muro	

Do you know any more related words which aren't in the list?

Introduction

Punctuation

Usage is the same in Spanish and English, but notice that inverted question and exclamation marks are placed at the beginning and end of the relevant sentence in Spanish.

¿Qué hora es?	*What's the time?*
¡Ten cuidado!	*Be careful!*
¡Socorro!	*Help!*

Notice too that at the beginning of a letter, a colon is used in Spanish, whereas a comma is preferred in English:

Querido José:	*Dear José,*

Focus and learn!

Most people make the excuse that they are no good at learning words as they have a poor memory. You don't! It is not your memory that is poor, it is failure to give it the guidance and focus it needs. In learning words from a list the learner has not yet decided when he or she is going to use them. There is no immediate goal.

To learn with least effort you need to have a set of clear goals. Choose your goals:

A I want to use the language to communicate with other speakers of that language:
  * on a business trip;
  * on a holiday trip;
  * on a social visit;
  * at home, for business reasons;
  * because I know someone I would like to talk to or write to.

B I want to be able to understand the language to:
  * read something in that language for pleasure, books, magazines, letters etc.;
  * read something for business, manuals, letters, faxes etc.;
  * listen to the radio;
  * watch television programmes;
  * read signs and instructions on a visit.

15

C I just enjoy learning languages.

You should choose the words and phrases, you are going to learn and focus on them and their meaning. Concentrating on the words and thinking about their meaning and the sound of them and looking for 'pegs' on which to 'hang' them (looking for related words, imaging them in pictures, remembering the sound of the words etc.) will help you to put them in your long term memory.

—— List of abbreviations used ——

(m.)	masculine noun
(f.)	feminine noun
(sing.)	singular form
(pl.)	plural form
(fam.)	familiar form of address
(form.)	formal/polite form of address

1 **Saludos** *Greetings*

Buenos días	*Good morning*	¿Qué tal?;	
Buenas tardes	*Good afternoon*	¿Qué hay?	*Hi!; How are you?*
Buenas tardes	*Good evening*	¿Cómo está?	
Buenas noches	*Good night* (greeting and taking leave)	(form.)	*How are you?*
		¿Cómo estás?	
		(fam.)	*How are you?*
Hola	*Hello*	Muy bien, gracias.	
Adiós	*Goodbye*	¿Y Usted?	*Very well, thank*
Hasta luego	*See you later*	(form.)	*you. And you?*
Hasta mañana	*See you tomorrow*	¿Y tú? (fam.)	*And you?*

¡OTRA VEZ!

● *Activity:* ¿Qué dirías? *What would you say?*

TRATAMIENTO
TITLES

formal titles used before first surname

Señor (Sr.)	*Mr; Sir*
Señora (Sra.)	*Mrs*
Señorita (Srta.)	*Miss*

Buenos días, Sr. López

formal titles used before first name

Don (D.)
Doña (Dña.)

Buenas tardes, Dña María

Usted (Vd.)	*you* (sing.)
Ustedes (Vds.)	*you* (pl.)

formal, polite forms of 'you'

2 Números *Numbers*

¡OTRA VEZ!

● *Activity:* ¿Qué dirías? *What would you say? (Look back to the previous page.)*

(a) Señor Suárez   (b) Conchita   (c) Doña María

NÚMEROS CARDINALES
CARDINAL NUMBERS

0	cero	20	veinte
1	uno (un), una	21	veintiuno (veintiún)
2	dos	22	veintidós
3	tres	30	treinta
4	cuatro	31	treinta y un(o)
5	cinco	40	cuarenta
6	seis	50	cincuenta
7	siete	60	sesenta
8	ocho	70	setenta
9	nueve	80	ochenta
10	diez	90	noventa
11	once	100	cien
12	doce	101	ciento uno
13	trece	500	quinientos (-as)
14	catorce	700	setecientos (-as)
15	quince	900	novecientos (-as)
16	dieciséis	1.000	mil
17	diecisiete	2.000	dos mil
18	dieciocho	1.000.000	un millón
19	diecinueve	2.000.000	dos millones

Notes on cardinal numbers

Numbers 1–30 are written as one word: 14: **catorce**; 22: **veintidós**.
Numbers 31–99 are written separately, with **y** between the tens and units:
33: **treinta y tres**; 67: **sesenta y siete**.
Y is not used, however, in numbers such as 101, 120, 1.067 etc.

2 Números *Numbers*

100 is written as **cien** when exactly 100 is intended: **Cien pesetas** = 100 pesetas.
More than 100 is **ciento**: 101 = **ciento uno**.
Multiples of **ciento** are regular: **doscientos**; **trescientos** etc., except: 500
quinientos; 700 **setecientos**; 900 **novecientos**.
Millón, as it is a noun, takes **de** when followed by a noun: **un millón de
coches**; **cinco millones de personas**.
Un is used instead of **uno** before masculine nouns: **veintiún días**;
veintiún años.

NÚMEROS ORDINALES
ORDINAL NUMBERS

primero-a	*first*
segundo-a	*second*
tercero-a	*third*
cuarto-a	*fourth*
quinto-a	*fifth*
sexto-a	*sixth*
séptimo-a	*seventh*
octavo-a	*eighth*
noveno-a	*ninth*
décimo-a	*tenth*

FRACCIONES
FRACTIONS

cuarto-a	*quarter*
medio-a	*half*
tres cuartos	*three quarters*
un kilo y medio	*a kilo and a half*
una vez	*once*
dos veces	*twice*
tres veces	*three times*

DECIMALES *DECIMALS*

A comma is used in Spanish instead of a point, and the numbers after the
decimal are not said individually as in English:
8,92   ocho coma noventa y dos
10,75   diez coma setenta y cinco

¡OTRA VEZ!

● *Activity:* Practica y lee estos números de teléfonos y sus prefijos.
Practise reading these telephone numbers and codes.

In Spain, numbers are said in pairs. 425788 would therefore be
cuarenta y dos, cincuenta y siete, ochenta y ocho. 463 would be
cuatro, sesenta y tres. 04 would be cero cuatro.

Try these:

93	217 62 92	(Barcelona)
91	732 80 44	(Madrid)
977	31 28 04	(Tarragona)
952	73 11 59	(Málaga)
945	15 99 01	(Vitoria)

What is your telephone number?

2 Números *Numbers*

¡OTRA VEZ!

● *Activity:*

1 Read these years aloud:

1.975	1.984
1.998	2.025

Add important dates in your own life and practise saying them:

Nací en . . .	*I was born in . . .*
Empecé a trabajar en . . .	*I started work in . . .*
Me casé en . . .	*I got married in . . .*
Fui a la universidad en . . .	*I went to university in . . .*

2 The Big Race: Where did they come?

Elena	Isabel	María

3 El calendario *The calendar*

EL CALENDARIO
THE CALENDAR

el día	*day*
la semana	*week*
la quincena	*fortnight*
el mes	*month*
el año	*year*
el año bisiesto	*leap year*

LOS DÍAS DE LA SEMANA
THE DAYS OF THE WEEK

lunes	*Monday*
martes	*Tuesday*
miércoles	*Wednesday*
jueves	*Thursday*
viernes	*Friday*
sábado	*Saturday*
domingo	*Sunday*

la mañana	*morning*
el mediodía	*midday*
la tarde	*afternoon; evening*
la noche	*night*
hoy	*today*
mañana	*tomorrow*
pasado mañana	*the day after tomorrow*
ayer	*yesterday*
anteayer	*the day before yesterday*
esta mañana	*this morning*
ayer por la tarde	*yesterday afternoon*
mañana por la tarde	*tomorrow evening*
el fin de semana	*the weekend*

LOS MESES
THE MONTHS

enero	*January*
febrero	*February*
marzo	*March*
abril	*April*
mayo	*May*
junio	*June*
julio	*July*
agosto	*August*
septiembre	*September*
octubre	*October*
noviembre	*November*
diciembre	*December*

In Spanish, the days of the week and months do not start with a capital letter.

DATES

Cardinal numbers (dos, tres, cuatro, etc.) are used for dates in Spanish, except for the first of each month (el primero).

el primero de enero	*1st January*
el dos de febrero	*2nd February*
el tres de marzo	*3rd March*
el veinte de abril	*20th April*

No preposition is used before the date:

Llegué el diez de noviembre.	*I arrived on the tenth of November.*

LAS CUATRO ESTACIONES
THE FOUR SEASONS

(en) invierno	*(in) winter*
(en) primavera	*(in) spring*
(en) verano	*(in) summer*
(en) otoño	*(in) autumn*

The seasons are masculine, except la primavera.

FIESTAS
HOLIDAYS

la Navidad	*Christmas*
la Semana Santa	*Easter / Holy Week*

3 El calendario *The calendar*

La Navidad

Christmas Eve (**Nochebuena**) is a more important day than Christmas Day in Spain. **Turrón** (*nougat*), **mazapán** (*marzipan cakes*) and **polvorones** (*shortbread cakes*) are traditional delicacies served at the end of the evening meal. Houses are decorated with a model crib (**Belén**) and sometimes with a Christmas tree. 'Merry Christmas' in Spanish is **Felices Navidades**. Children traditionally receive their presents from the Three Kings on January 6.

La Semana Santa

Holy Week is an important celebration throughout Spain. Statues of saints, virgins or scenes from the crucifixion are carried through the streets on floats (**pasos**), lit by candles and usually accompanied by music. The processions in Sevilla and Valladolid are particularly famous.

Días de Fiesta *National Public Holidays*

1° de enero	Día de Año Nuevo	New Year's Day
6 de enero	Día de los Reyes Magos	Epiphany
1° de mayo	Fiesta del Trabajo	Labour Day
25 de julio	Día de Santiago	St James' Day (Patron Saint of Spain)
12 de octubre	Día de la Hispanidad	Columbus Day
1° de noviembre	Todos los Santos	All Saint's Day
6 de diciembre	Día de la Constitución	Constitution Day

In addition to these national holidays, Spain has various holidays particular to individual regions.

Las Fallas take place on March 19 in Valencia. Models satirising political and other public figures are ceremonially burnt in the main squares.

La Feria de Abril is an annual event in Sevilla. It is a week-long celebration of flamenco costumes and dancing, horse riding and sherry.

San Fermín is a fiesta held in Pamplona from the 6th to the 15th of July. It is especially famous for the **encierros**, when bulls run free through the streets and locals and tourists test their courage by running in front of them.

3 El calendario *The calendar*

¡OTRA VEZ!

● *Activity:*

1 ¿Cuándo son los cumpleaños?   Say when the birthdays are:
  (cumpleaños   =   birthday)

  ¿Cuándo es tu (fam.)/su (form.)
  cumpleaños?   When is your birthday?

  Mi cumpleaños es el . . .   My birthday is . . .
  El cumpleaños de mi madre/   My mother's/father's birthday
  padre es el . . .   is . . .
  El cumpleaños de mi hija/   My daughter's/son's
  hijo es el . . .   birthday is . . .

2 ¿Cuándo son las reuniones?   When are the meetings?

(a) 10 JAN   (b) 16 MAR   (c) 22 JUN   (d) 1 OCT   (e) 15 NOV

¿Cuántos días hay en una semana?   *How many days are there in a week?*
¿Cuántas semanas hay en un mes?   *How many weeks are there in a month?*
¿Cuántos meses hay en un año?   *How many months are there in a year?*

4 El reloj *The clock*

¿QUÉ HORA ES?
WHAT TIME IS IT?

Es . . .	*It is . . .*
la una en punto	*one o'clock*
la una y cinco	*five past one*
la una y media	*half past one*
Son . . .	*It is . . .*
las dos y diez	*ten past two*
las dos y cuarto	*quarter past two*
las dos y veinte	*twenty past two*
las dos y media	*half past two*
las tres menos cuarto	*quarter to three*
la tres menos diez	*ten to three*
las tres en punto	*three o'clock*

La hora digital

las trece cero siete	*13.07*
las quince diecinueve	*15.19*
las diecinueve cincuenta y cuatro	*19.54*
las veintidós cuarenta y siete	*22.47*

la mañana	*morning*
la tarde	*afternoon; early evening*
la noche	*night*
¿Tiene hora? (form.)	*Have you got the time?*
¿Tienes hora? (fam.)	*Have you got the time?*
¿A qué hora?	*At what time?*
a las diez en punto de la mañana	*at ten o'clock in the morning*
a las cinco de la tarde	*at five o'clock in the afternoon*
el mediodía	*midday*
la medianoche	*midnight*
el reloj	*clock; watch*
la correa del reloj	*watchstrap*

Mi reloj adelanta/atrasa.	*My watch is fast / slow.*
Lo siento, llego tarde.	*Sorry I'm late.*
Mi reloj no funciona/está roto.	*My watch doesn't work / is broken.*
He perdido mi reloj.	*I have lost my watch.*
Necesito una pila nueva para mi reloj.	*I need a new battery for my watch.*

4 El reloj *The clock*

'am' is expressed by **de la mañana.**

son las diez de la mañana   *It's 10am.*

'pm' is expressed by **de la tarde** for the afternoon and evening and by **de la noche** for later hours:

Son las cinco de la tarde.   *It's 5pm.*
Son las once y media de la noche. *It's 11.30pm.*

por la mañana   *in the morning*
por la tarde   *in the afternoon / early evening*
por la noche   *at night*

If no specific time is mentioned, one of the above may be used.

¡OTRA VEZ!

● *Activity:* Dí a qué hora es la cita. *Practise saying these times:*

¿A qué hora quedamos?   *When shall we meet?*
¿Qué tal a la/las . . .?   *What about at . . .?*

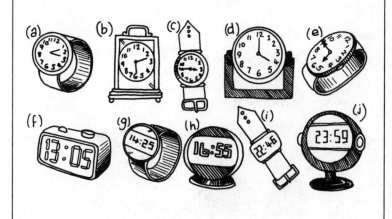

25

5 Los colores *Colours*

amarillo-a	*yellow*	rojo-a	*red*
azul	*blue*	rosa	*pink*
azul celeste	*light blue*	turquesa	*turquoise*
azul marino	*navy blue*	verde	*green*
beige	*beige*	violeta	*violet*
blanco-a	*white*		
dorado-a	*gold(en)*	oscuro	*dark*
gris	*grey*	claro	*light; pale*
marrón	*brown*	vivo	*bright*
morado-a	*purple*	fluorescente	*fluorescent*
naranja	*orange*		
negro-a	*black*	verde claro	*light green*
plateado-a	*silver*	verde oscuro	*dark green*

Colours are adjectives and must therefore agree in number and, if they end in **-o**, in gender with the noun they qualify: e.g. **la** camisa blanc**a**; **el** coche negr**o**; **los** ojos azul**es**.

Note that some colours have the same form for masculine and feminine nouns: e.g. **el** gato **gris**; **la** camisa **gris**.

¡OTRA VEZ!

● *Activity:*

1 ¿De qué color quieres que sean?
What colours would you like them to be?
Describe los jerseys y los pantalones.
Describe the jerseys and trousers.

2 ¿De qué color son los banderas?
What colours are the flags of the following countries?
USA; UK; Italy; France; Germany; Spain

26

6 Adjetivos *Adjectives*

ADJECTIVES

You can use these words to say something about or describe things, people, places, or feelings. You will also find appropriate adjectives included in the topic areas.

Spanish adjectives usually come after the noun they are describing and always agree in gender and number with it.

abierto-a	*open*	doble	*double*
aburrido-a	*boring; bored*	domesticado-a	*tame*
activo-a	*active*	dulce	*soft; sweet*
afectuoso-a	*warm*	duro-a	*hard; difficult*
afilado-a	*sharp*	educado-a	*polite*
alto-a	*tall; high*	en forma	*fit*
alto-a	*loud*	enfermo-a	*ill*
amable	*friendly*	equivocado-a	*wrong*
amargo-a	*bitter*	estrecho-a	*narrow*
ancho-a	*wide*	estúpido-a	*stupid*
animado-a	*lively*	extenso-a	*wide*
antiguo-a	*old; ancient*	fácil	*easy*
antipático-a	*unfriendly*	falso-a	*false*
áspero-a	*rough*	famoso-a	*famous*
bajo-a	*low; short*	feo-a	*ugly*
barato-a	*cheap*	frágil	*fragile*
bien	*well*	fresco-a	*fresh; cool*
blando-a	*soft*	frío-a	*cold*
bonito-a	*nice*	fuerte	*strong*
bueno-a	*good*	generoso-a	*generous*
caliente	*hot; warm*	gordo-a	*fat*
cansado-a	*tired*	grande	*big*
caro-a	*expensive*	gratis	*free (no cost)*
cercano-a	*nearby; near*	grosero-a	*rude*
ciego-a	*blind*	guapo	*handsome*
claro-a	*clear; light*	holgazán-ana	*idle*
cobarde	*cowardly*	horrible	*horrible*
cojo-a	*lame*	imposible	*impossible*
complicado-a	*complicated*	ingenioso-a	*clever*
contento-a	*happy*	inocente	*innocent*
correcto-a	*right; correct*	inteligente	*intelligent*
corriente	*common*	interesante	*interesting*
culpable	*guilty*	joven	*young*
débil	*weak*	justo-a	*fair (decision)*
delgado-a	*thin*	largo-a	*long*
divertido-a	*fun*	lejano-a	*far*

6 Adjetivos *Adjectives*

lento-a	*slow*	profundo-a	*deep*
libre	*free (not occupied)*	querido-a	*dear (beloved)*
limpio-a	*clean*	rápido-a	*quick*
lindo-a	*pretty*	raro-a	*strange; rare*
listo-a	*ready*	salvaje	*wild*
lleno-a	*full*	seco-a	*dry*
malo-a	*bad*	sencillo-a	*easy; single*
minusválido-a	*handicapped*		*(ticket, room)*
moderno-a	*modern*	simpático-a	*friendly*
mojado-a	*wet*	sordo-a	*deaf*
muerto-a	*dead*	suave	*soft*
nuevo-a	*new*	sucio-a	*dirty*
ocupado-a	*busy*	tacaño-a	*mean*
ocupado-a	*occupied (engaged)*	tarde	*late*
oscuro-a	*dark*	templado-a	*warm*
pasado-a	*last (last week)*	temprano-a	*early*
pasivo-a	*passive*	terrible	*terrible*
pequeño-a	*small*	tierno-a	*tender*
perezoso-a	*lazy*	tranquilo-a	*quiet; calm*
pesado-a	*heavy; boring*	triste	*sad*
plano-a	*flat*	último-a	*last; latest*
poco amable	*unfriendly*	vacío-a	*empty*
poco profundo-a	*shallow*	valiente	*brave*
posible	*possible*	verdadero-a	*true*
precioso-a	*beautiful*	viejo-a	*old*
primero-a	*first*	vivo-a	*alive*

¡OTRA VEZ!

● Activity: Choose any twelve words from the list and write them down here, and then write down their opposites beside them.

bueno - malo   *good - bad*

_____   _____

_____   _____

_____   _____

_____   _____

_____   _____

7 Adverbios *Adverbs*

ahora	*now, just now*	mal	*badly*
antes	*before*	más	*more*
alto	*loudly*	menos	*less*
bajo	*softly*	mucho	*much; many*
bastante	*rather*	muy	*very*
bastante;		poco	*little; few*
suficiente	*enough*	por lo menos	*at least*
bien	*well*	por término	
casi	*almost*	medio	*on average*
claramente	*clearly*	precisamente	*exactly, precisely*
completamente	*completely*	probablemente	*probably*
demasiado	*too (much; many)*	quizá	*perhaps*
desgraciadamente	*unfortunately*	realmente	*really*
especialmente	*specially*	solamente	*only*
exactamente	*exactly*	también	*also*
lentamente	*slowly*	totalmente	*completely*

¡OTRA VEZ!

● Activity: Modify these sentences by adding a word in the gaps:

Marta es _____ alta.   Marta is _____ tall.
Estoy _____ cansado.   I am _____ tired.
Mis hermanas cantan _____ .   My sisters sing _____ .
Hace _____ calor.   It is _____ hot.
Tengo _____ dinero.   I've got _____ money.

8 ¿Dónde? *Where?*

a	*to*	en casa	*at home*
a la izquierda	*on the left*	en el centro (de)	*in the middle of*
a la derecha	*on the right*	en lo alto (de)	*at the top of*
a través (de)	*through*	en ninguna parte	*nowhere*
abajo	*down*	en todas partes	*everywhere*
adelante	*forward*	encima (de)	*above*
ahí	*there*	enfrente (de)	*opposite*
al fondo (de)	*at the end of*	entre	*between*
alrededor (de)	*around*	fuera (de)	*outside*
aquí	*here*	hacia	*towards*
arriba	*up*	junto a	*beside*
cerca (de)	*near*	lejos (de)	*far from*
debajo (de)	*under*	más allá (de)	*beyond*
delante (de)	*in front of*	por delante	*past*
dentro (de)	*in*	por encima (de)	*over*
detrás (de)	*behind*	posterior,	
en	*in, at, on*	de atrás	*back*
en alguna parte	*somewhere*	sobre	*on*

¡OTRA VEZ!

● Activity: ¿Dónde está Alberto? *Where's Alberto?*

(a) (b) (c) MGM (d)

30

9 ¿Cuándo? *When?*

actualmente	*nowadays*	luego	*next*
alguna vez,		mañana	*tomorrow*
a veces	*sometimes*	más tarde	*afterwards, later*
antes de	*before*	mientras	*while*
aún (más)	*still (more)*	nunca	*never*
ayer	*yesterday*	otra vez	*again*
con frecuencia,		por lo general	*usually*
a menudo	*often*	primero	*first*
de vez en cuando	*from time to time*	pronto	*soon*
después	*after*	recientemente	*recently*
el año pasado	*last year*	siempre	*always*
entonces	*then*	tan pronto como	*as soon as*
entre tanto	*meanwhile*	tarde	*late*
este año	*this year*	temprano	*early*
finalmente	*finally*	todavía	*still*
hace	*ago*	último-a	*last*
hasta	*until*	una vez	*once*
hoy	*today*	ya	*already*
inmediatamente	*immediately*		

¡OTRA VEZ!

● *Activity: Add a word to complete these sentences and their translations:*

1) Vamos _____ a España de vacaciones.
   We _____ go to Spain for our holidays.

2) Vamos a ir _____ al centro.
   _____ *we are going to the centre.*

3) _____ fuimos a otro restaurante.
   _____ *we went to another restaurant.*

4) _____ hace buen tiempo pero _____ llueve.
   _____ *the weather is good but* _____ *it rains.*

31

10 Pronombres interrogativos *Question words*

¿Cómo?	*How?*	¿De dónde?	*Where from?*
¿Cómo estás?	*How are you?*	¿De dónde eres?	*Where are you from?*
¿Cuándo?	*When?*	¿A dónde?	*Where to?*
¿Cuándo es la fiesta?	*When is the party?*	¿A dónde vamos?	*Where shall we go?*
¿Cuánto?	*How much?*	¿Por qué?	*Why?*
¿Cuánto dinero tienes?	*How much money have you got?*	¿Por qué llegas tarde?	*Why are you late?*
¿Cuántos-as?	*How many?*	¿Qué?	*What?*
¿Cuántos coches tienen?	*How many cars have they got?*	¿Qué es esto?	*What is this?*
¿Cuál?	*Which?*	¿Quién?	*Who?*
¿Cuál te gusta?	*Which one do you like?*	¿Quién eres?	*Who are you?*
¿Dónde?	*Where?*	¿Qué clase de . . . ?	*What kind of . . . ?*
¿Dónde quedamos?	*Where shall we meet?*	¿Qué clase de música te gusta?	*What kind of music do you like?*

¡OTRA VEZ!

● *Activity: What was the question?*

Por ejemplo:

Respuesta:	*Answer:*
Son las dos y media.	*It's half past two.*
Pregunta:	*Question:*
¿Qué hora es?	*What time is it?*

Preguntas:	Respuestas:
1 ¿_____?	2.000 pesetas
2 ¿_____?	Sr. Álvarez.
3 ¿_____?	Un Citroën
4 ¿_____?	En el jardín.
5 ¿_____?	Bien, gracias.

11 Artículos, adjetivos demostrativos y posesivos, pronombres y conjunciones
Articles, demonstrative and possessive adjectives, pronouns and conjunctions

Artículo determinado   *The definite article*

el; la; los; las	*the*

Artículo indeterminado   *The indefinite article*

un; una	*a*	unos, unas	*some*

Adjetivos demostrativos   *Demonstrative adjectives*

este; esta	*this*	estos; estas	*these*
eso; esa	*that*	esos; esas	*those*

Adjetivos posesivos   *Possessive adjectives*

mi (s)	*my*	mío-a (s)	*mine*
tu (s)	*your*	tuyo-a (s)	*yours* (fam.)
su (s)	*his, her, its,* *your* (form.)	suyo-a (s)	*his, her, its,* *yours* (form.)
nuestro-a (s)	*our*	nuestro-a (s)	*ours*
vuestro-a (s)	*your*	vuestro-a (s)	*yours*
sus	*their*	suyo-a (s)	*theirs, yours* (form. pl)

The forms mío/a, tuyo/a etc., can follow a noun:

un amigo mío	*a (male) friend of mine*
una colega mía	*a (female) colleage of mine*

or if used after a verb, the definite article is placed in front:

esta oficina es la mía	*this office is mine*
este billete es el tuyo	*this ticket is yours*

Pronombres sujeto   *Subject pronouns*

yo	*I*	nosotros-as	*we*
tú	*you* (fam.)	vosotros-as	*you* (fam. pl.)
usted	*you* (form.)	ustedes	*you* (form. pl.)
él	*he*	ellos-as	*they*
ella	*she*		

(Refer to Section 1 – *Greetings and Titles*, page 17.)

In Spanish, the subject pronouns are not often used for verbs whose endings show who or what the subject is. For example, it is not necessary to say **Yo soy de Londres** (*I am from London*) but simply **Soy de Londres**, as **soy** can only refer to *I*.

Use **tú** when addressing children, friends, young people, relatives or when invited to do so. Otherwise, use **usted**.

Preposition forms:

menos yo	*except me*	para tí	*for you*
de tu parte	*from you*	para él	*for him*
para mí	*for me*	para ella	*for her*

para nosotros-as	*for us*	consigo	*with him / herself*
		con él	*with him*
conmigo	*with me*	sin ellos-as	*without them*
contigo	*with you* (fam.)		

Pronombres complemento *Object pronouns*

These can be direct (**Lo** haré – *I'll do it*) or indirect (¿Qué **me** recomienda? – *What do you recommend to me?*)

me	*me / to me*	nos	*us / to us*
te	*you / to you* (fam.)	os	*you / to you* (fam. pl.)
le	*you / to you* (form.)	les	*you / to you*
	him / to him		(form. pl.)
la	*her / to her*		*them / to them*
	it / to it (fem.)	las	*them / to them* (fem.)
lo	*him / to him*	los	*them / to them* (masc.)

Conjunciones *Conjunctions*

aunque	*although*	o	*or*
cuando	*when*	si	*if*
pero	*but*	y	*and*
porque	*because*		

¿**Me** llama a las siete?	*Will you call me at 7?*
¿**Me** trae la cuenta?	*Could you bring me the bill?*
¿**Me** dice la hora?	*Could you tell me the time?*
¿Puede ayudar**me**?	*Could you help me?*
Necesito **un** plano de Madrid	*I need a street plan of Madrid*
¿Dónde está **la** salida?	*Where is the exit?*
Él es inglés	*He is English*
Lo/la compro	*I'll buy it*
Este es **mi** pasaporte	*This is my passport*
¿Dónde está **el tuyo**?	*Where's yours?*
María es una amiga **mía**	*Maria is a friend of mine*
Nos gusta viajar **pero** ...	*We like travelling but ...*
Nos da miedo el avión	*We're afraid of flying*
Para mí, ensalada **y** pollo	*For me, salad and chicken*

¡OTRA VEZ!

● Activity: Put the right form of: **1** this/these **2** my **3** our

in front of these words:

libro; libros; casa; casas; coche; familia; restaurante

12 Verbos *Verbs*

There are three categories of Spanish verbs, according to the ending of the infinitive: either **-ar**, **-er** or **-ir** (**hablar** – *to speak*, **comer** – *to eat*, **vivir** – *to live*). Some verbs are regular, which means they follow a set pattern, whereas others are irregular, as they deviate from this pattern in places. This deviation usually takes the form of a vowel change in the middle of the word, or occasionally the first person singular in the present tense has a distinct form (e.g.: **doy**, **digo**, **hago**– *I give, I say, I do*).

In some respects Spanish verbs are more complicated than English verbs, as there is a separate form for each person and for the singular and plural. However, in Spanish there is no equivalent of 'do/does' or 'did'; negatives are formed simply by adding **no** before the verbs e.g.

No fumo.   *I don't smoke.*

and verbs in questions have the same form as the affirmative, e.g.

¿Dónde vives?   *Where do you live?*

In compound tenses, the auxiliary verb **haber** is used together with the past participle:

Este verano he viajado por el   *This summer I travelled around*
   Norte de España.   *the north of Spain.*
¿Has visto mi libro?   *Have you seen my book?*

For more about verb formation and endings, see *Teach Yourself Spanish Verbs.*

MAIN VERB TENSES

Presente
Viajo mucho.

Present
I travel a lot.

Pretérito indefinido
Viajé a España en 1992.

Past
I went to Spain in 1992.

Pretérito perfecto.
He viajado mucho.

Perfect
I have travelled a lot.

Pretérito imperfecto
Antes viajaba mucho.

Imperfect
I used to travel a lot.

Futuro
Viajaré a Asturias en mayo.

The future
I'll go to Asturias in May.

12 Verbos *Verbs*

SER *AND* ESTAR
TO BE

The verb 'to be' is expressed in Spanish either by **ser** or **estar**. These verbs are not interchangeable and both are irregular.

Ser

Ser is used in the following situations:

Name	Soy María López.	*I am María Lopez.*
Nationality	Soy inglés.	*I am English.*
Origin	Es de Londres.	*He / she / it is from London.*
Occupation	Soy médico.	*I am a doctor.*
Possession	Es mi coche.	*It's my car.*
Time	¿Qué hora es?	*What time is it?*
Date	Hoy es el 10 de agosto.	*Today is the 10th of August.*
	Es martes.	*It's Tuesday.*
Price	¿Cuánto es?	*How much is it?*
	Son 1000 pesetas.	*It's 1000 pesetas.*
Quantity	Es suficiente/mucho.	*It's enough / a lot.*
Size	Es pequeño-a/grande.	*It's small / big.*
Height	Es bajo-a/alto-a.	*It's short / tall.*

Ser is also used when talking about political or religious persuasion.

Estar

Estar is used with a preposition or adverb to indicate:

Location	Estoy en el bar.	*I'm in the bar.*
Position	Está cerca.	*It's near.*

It is also used for moods, well-being and state of health:

¿Cómo estás?	*How are you?*
Estoy bien, gracias.	*I'm fine, thanks.*

With an adjective, **estar** also expresses a temporary state or quality:

Está libre.	*It's free.*
Está cerrado hoy.	*It's closed today.*
Está completo.	*It's full.*

TENER *TO HAVE*

Tener is used to express age:

¿Cuántos años tienes?	*How old are you?*
Tengo doce años.	*I am 12.*

To talk about your family:

Tengo dos hermanas.	*I've got two sisters.*
¿Tienes hijos?	*Have you got any children?*

To talk about your possessions:

Tengo un coche viejo.	*I've got an old car.*

It is also used in several idiomatic expressions:

Tengo ...	*I'm ...*
frío	*cold*
calor	*hot*
hambre	*hungry*
sed	*thirsty*
miedo	*afraid*
sueño	*sleepy*
prisa	*in a hurry*
razón	*right*

Other expressions which use **tener** are:

¿Tiene hora?	*Have you got the time?*
Aquí tiene.	*Here you are.*
Tengo una habitación reservada.	*I have a room reserved.*

Note that **tener que + infinitive** expresses the idea of obligation:

Tengo que llamar por teléfono.	*I have to make a phone call.*

IR *TO GO*

¿Adónde vas?	*Where are you going?*
Voy a la playa	*I'm going to the beach*

Ir + a + infinitive is used to express the immediate future:

¿Qué vas a hacer este verano?	*What are you going to do this summer?*

12 Verbos *Verbs*

Voy a ir a Francia.	*I'm going to France.*
Voy a visitar a mi hermano.	*I'm going to visit my brother.*

HAY *THERE IS/ARE*

¿Dónde hay una parada de taxis?	*Where is there a taxi rank?*
Hay dos supermercados	*There are two supermarkets*
¿Hay una mesa libre?	*Is there a free table?*
¿Hay una plaza en este tren?	*Is there a seat on this train?*

Hay is used in the greeting:

¡Hola, Pedro! ¿Qué hay?	*Hello Pedro. How're things?*

Hay can also be used to express obligation or necessity:

Hay que tomar el sol con precaución.	*You must be careful when you're sunbathing.*
Hay que estar en el aeropuerto una hora antes del vuelo.	*You must be at the airport an hour before the flight.*

USEFUL VERB COMBINATIONS

The following expressions can be combined with the infinitive of both regular and irregular verbs (without an additional preposition):

Quisiera/quisiéramos ...	*I / we would like ...*
Quisiera alquilar un coche.	*I would like to rent a car.*
Voy/vamos a ...	*I / we are going to ...*
Vamos a llegar a las cinco.	*We'll be arriving at 5.*
Me/nos gustaría ...	*I / we would like (to) ...*
Me gustaría tomar café.	*I'd like to have a coffee.*
Tengo/tenemos que ...	*I / we have to ...*
Tengo que trabajar mañana.	*I've got to work tomorrow.*
Prefiero/preferimos ...	*I / we prefer ...*
Prefiero el vino tinto.	*I prefer red wine.*
Debo/debemos ...	*I / we must / ought to ...*
Debemos salir pronto.	*We must leave early.*
Espero/esperamos ...	*I / we hope to ...*
Espero terminar el informe pronto.	*I hope to finish the report soon.*

12 Verbos *Verbs*

Hay que . . .	*You must / it is necessary to . . .*
Hay que comprobar el aceite.	*It's necessary to check the oil.*
¿Se puede . . .?	*Is it possible to . . .?*
¿Se puede aparcar aquí?	*Is it possible to park here?*

1 Asuntos personales *Personal matters*

EL ASPECTO PERSONAL
PERSONAL APPEARANCE

Soy ...	*I am ...*
El/Ella es ...	*He / she is ...*
alto-a	*tall*
bajo-a	*short*
de estatura mediana	*medium height*
delgado-a	*thin*
fuerte	*well built*
gordo-a	*fat*

Tengo el pelo ...	*I have ... hair*
blanco	*white*
caoba	*auburn*
castaño	*chestnut*
claro	*fair*
corto	*short*
gris	*grey*
lacio	*straight*
largo	*long*
ondulado	*wavy*
oscuro	*dark*
pelirrojo	*red*
rizado	*curly*
rubio	*blond*

y los ojos ...	*and ... eyes*
azules	*blue*
azul-grises	*blue-grey*
marrones	*brown*
negros	*black*
verdes	*green*

Soy miope/hipermétrope.	*I am short / long sighted.*
Llevo gafas	*I wear glasses*
Llevo lentillas	*I wear contact lenses*

Soy ...	*I am ...*
bien parecido-a	*good looking*
guapo-a	*handsome*

el peso	*weight*
Peso ... kgs.	*I weigh ... kgs.*
Soy de piel ...	*I am ... skinned*
blanca	*fair*
morena	*dark*
pálida	*pale*
Estoy bronceado-a.	*I'm suntanned.*
El/ella tiene ...	*He / she has ...*
acné	*acne*
arrugas	*wrinkles*
barba	*a beard*
bigote	*a moustache*
la boca ancha	*a wide mouth*
la boca pequeña	*a narrow mouth*
una bonita sonrisa	*a nice smile*
las cejas pobladas	*bushy eyebrows*
una cicatriz	*a scar*
la curva de la felicidad	*a beer belly*
un grano/granos	*a spot / spots*
la frente despejada	*a high forehead*
hoyüelos	*dimples*
los labios carnosos/finos	*thick / thin lips*
un lunar	*a mole*
una mancha de nacimiento	*a birth mark*
las orejas grandes/pequeñas	*big / small ears*
pecas	*freckles*
la nariz aguileña	*a Roman nose*
chata	*a button nose*
de boxeador	*a boxer's nose*
grande	*a big nose*
respingona	*an upturned nose*
torcida	*broken nose*
Está calvo.	*He is bald.*
El/ella es ...	*He / she is ...*
feo-a	*ugly*
guapo-a	*handsome,beautiful*
mono-a/lindo-a	*sweet / cute*

1 Asuntos personales *Personal matters*

El/ella está . . .	*He / she is . . .*
bien arreglado-a	*well groomed*
desaliñado-a	*scruffy*
limpio-a	*clean*
sucio-a	*dirty*

| ¡Qué guapa! | *She's really beautiful.* |
| ¡El no está nada mal tampoco! | *He's not bad either!* |

¡OTRA VEZ!

● *Activity:* ¿Cómo eres? *What are you like?*

Estoy _____   I am _____

_____   _____

Soy _____   I am _____

_____   _____

Tengo _____   I have _____

_____   _____

1 **Asuntos personales** *Personal matters*

EL CURRICULUM VITAE

Mi Curriculum Vitae *My CV*

Nombre	*First Name*
Apellido	*Surname*
Edad	*Age*
Estado civil	*Married / single*
Fecha de nacimiento	*Date of birth*
Lugar de nacimiento	*Place of birth*
Nacionalidad	*Nationality*
Estudios	*Education*
Experiencia	*Experience*
Aficiones	*Interests*

SENTIMIENTOS Y EMOCIONES
FEELINGS AND EMOTIONS

la alegría	*happiness; joy*
la compasión	*compassion*
el descontento	*dissatisfaction*
la emoción	*emotion*
el entusiasmo	*enthusiasm*
el (buen/mal) humor	*(good / bad) mood*
el miedo	*fear*
la satis-facción	*satisfaction*
el senti-miento	*feeling*
la simpatía	*sympathy*
el terror	*dread*
la tristeza	*sadness*

Estoy . . .	*I am / feel . . .*
aburrido-a	*bored*
agotado-a	*drained*
alegre	*happy*
apenado-a	*distressed*
asqueado-a	*disgusted*
avergonzado-a	*ashamed*
cansado-a	*tired*
contentísimo-a	*overjoyed*
contento-a	*happy*
deprimido-a	*depressed*
descontento-a	*dissatisfied*
encantado-a	*delighted*
enfermo-a/bien	*ill / well*
en forma	*fit*
hablador-a	*talkative*
hecho polvo	*shattered; exhausted*
horrorizado-a	*appalled*
inquieto-a	*apprehensive*

1 **Asuntos personales** *Personal matters*

mejor/peor	*better / worse*
molesto-a	*annoyed*
preocupado-a	*concerned; worried*
rendido-a	*exhausted*
sorprendido-a	*surprised*
triste	*sad*

Me siento . . .	*I am / feel . . .*
animado-a	*lively*
defraudado-a	*let down*
de maravilla	*great!*
emocionado-a	*emotional*
entusiasta	*enthusiastic*
fabuloso-a	*terrific*
fatal	*terrible*
optimista	*hopeful*
rechazado-a	*rejected*
relajado-a	*relaxed; laid back*
sexy	*sexy*
violento-a	*violent*

Tengo . . .	*I am / feel . . .*
alegría	*happy*
curiosidad	*curious*
envidia	*envy*
hambre	*hungry*
miedo	*frightened*
sed	*thirsty*
sueño	*sleepy*
temor	*afraid*

¿Cómo te encuentras?	*How are you feeling?*
Estoy de buen/mal humor.	*I am in a good / bad mood.*

El/ella está . . .	*He / she is . . .*
sonriendo	*smiling*
llorando	*crying*

1 Asuntos personales *Personal matters*

CARACTERÍSTICAS
CHARACTERISTICS

¿Qué clase de persona eres?	*What sort of a person are you?*
Soy...	*I am...*
abierto-a; franco-a	*open; frank*
aburrido-a	*boring*
afable	*pleasant*
alegre	*cheerful*
amable	*gentle; friendly*
ambicioso-a	*ambitious*
antipático-a	*nasty; unfriendly*
arrogante	*arrogant*
astuto-a	*cunning*
atento-a	*considerate*
avaricioso-a	*greedy*
callado-a	*quiet*
cariñoso-a	*affectionate*
celoso-a	*jealous*
compasivo-a	*sympathetic*
confiado-a	*confident*
cruel	*cruel*
curioso-a	*curious*
de confianza	*trustworthy*
despistado-a	*absent minded*
despótico-a	*overbearing*
diestro-a/ zurdo-a	*right-handed / left-handed*
diplomático-a	*tactful*
divertido-a	*humorous; fun*
educado-a	*polite*
egoísta	*selfish*
encantador-a	*charming*
envidioso-a	*envious*
estúpido-a	*stupid*
feliz	*happy*
formal	*well behaved*
generoso-a	*generous*
gracioso-a	*funny*
grosero-a	*rude*

honorado-a	*honest*
impaciente	*impatient*
inculto-a	*rough*
ingenuo-a	*naive*
inocente	*innocent*
insolente	*insolent*
inteligente	*intelligent*
irresponsable	*irresponsible*
juicioso-a	*wise*
modesto-a	*modest*
nervioso-a	*nervous*
obstinado-a	*obstinate*
ordinario-a	*coarse; vulgar*
orgulloso-a	*proud*
paciente	*patient*
perezoso-a	*lazy*
precavido-a	*cautious*
presumido-a	*boastful*
prudente	*prudent*
raro-a	*strange*
razonable	*reasonable*
refinado-a	*refined*
rencoroso-a	*spiteful*
reservado-a	*reserved*
respetable	*respectable*
reticente	*reticent*
sagaz	*shrewd*
sensible	*sensitive*
serio-a	*serious*
servicial	*helpful*
sigiloso-a	*secretive*
simpático-a	*friendly*
sincero-a	*sincere*
tacaño-a	*miserly*
tímido-a	*timid*
tolerante	*tolerant*
torpe	*clumsy; dim witted*
trabajador-a	*hard-working*
travieso-a	*mischievous*
valeroso-a	*courageous*
valiente	*brave*
vengativo-a	*vindictive*
violento-a	*violent*

1 Asuntos personales *Personal matters*

GUSTOS Y PREFERENCIAS
LIKES AND DISLIKES

Me gusta-n	*I like*
No me gusta-n	*I don't like*
Me gustaría	*I would like*
Prefiero	*I prefer*
Me encanta-n	*I love*

aborrecer	*to abhor*
admirar	*to admire*
adorar	*to adore*
despreciar	*to despise*
odiar	*to hate*
ser aficionado-a a	*to be fond of*
ser entusiasta de	*to be a fan of*

Note the structure of the verbs **gustar** and **encantar**.

Me gusta el vino.	*I like wine.*
	(lit. Wine is pleasing to me.)
Me gustan los gatos.	*I like cats.*

Similarly:

Me encanta la música.	*I love music.*

To form the negative, **no** is placed at the beginning of the sentence:

No me gusta el café.	*I don't like coffee.*

To talk about somebody else's likes and dislikes, use **le/les** (form.) before **gusta (-n)**. (See page 32 for more help with indirect pronouns.)

1 Asuntos personales *Personal matters*

¡OTRA VEZ!

● *Activity:* **1** ¿Qué te gusta? *What do you like?*
Example: Me gusta el café – *I like coffee.*

_____

_____

_____

2 ¿Cuales son sus gustos? *What are his likes and dislikes?*
Example: Le gusta el vino – *He likes wine.*

LA FAMILIA
FAMILY

el árbol genealógico	*family tree*	los parientes cercanos	*close relations*
los parientes	*relations*	los parientes lejanos	*distant relations*

1 **Asuntos personales** *Personal matters*

materno;	*maternal;*
por parte	*on the mother's*
de madre	*side of the family*
paterno;	*paternal;*
por parte	*on the father's*
de padre	*side*
los bisabuelos	*great grandparents*
la bisabuela	*great grandmother*
el bisabuelo	*great grandfather*
los abuelos	*grandparents*
la abuela	*grandmother*
la abuelita	*grandma*
el abuelo	*grandfather*
el abuelito	*grandpa*
el nieto/la nieta	*grandson / daughter*
los padres	*parents*
la madre	*mother*
la mamá	*mum*
la madrasta	*stepmother*
la suegra	*mother-in-law*
el padre	*father*
el papá	*dad*
el padrastro	*stepfather*
el suegro	*father-in-law*

el tío	*uncle*
la tía	*aunt*
el hijo	*son*
el yerno	*son-in-law*
la hija	*daughter*
la nuera	*daughter-in-law*
el hermano	*brother*
los hermanos	*brothers and sisters*
el cuñado	*brother-in-law*
la hermana	*sister*
la cuñada	*sister-in-law*
el hermanastro	*half-brother*
la hermanastra	*half-sister*
el primo/la prima	*cousin*
el/la adulto-a	*adult*
el/la adolescente	*adolescent*
el/la joven	*teenager*
el/la niño-a	*child*
los niños	*children*
el bebé	*baby*
los padrinos	*godparents*
la madrina	*godmother*
el padrino	*godfather*
el/la ahijado-a	*godchild*

Me gusta/No me gusta (alguien)	*I like / dislike (someone)*
Me llevo bien/mal con (alguien)	*I get on well / badly with (someone)*
No aguanto a (alguien)	*I can't stand (someone)*

los/las	
gemelos-as	*identical twins*
el hermano	
mayor	*older brother*
la hermana	
menor	*younger sister*
el/la hijo-a	
único-a	*only child*
el/la huérfano-a	*orphan*
el matrimonio	*married couple*

los/las	
mellizos-as	*twins*
adoptado-a	*adopted*
una fotografía	*photograph*
un álbum	
de fotos	*photograph album*
Esta es una	*Here is a photo*
foto de mi ...	*of my ...*

LOS ANIMALES DOMÉSTICOS
PETS

¡Cuidado con el perro!
Beware of the dog!

el perro	dog
el caniche	poodle
el labrador	labrador
el pastor alemán	alsatian
el pastor escocés/ el collie	collie
el perro de caza	hunting dog
el perro guardián	guard dog
el perro-guía	guide dog
el cesto del perro	dog box; basket
el collar	collar
la comida	food
la correa	lead
el hueso	bone
la caca de perro	dog dirt

el canario	canary
el pájaro	bird
el periquito	budgerigar
la jaula	cage
el alpiste	birdseed
el pez de colores	gold fish
el pez tropical	tropical fish
el acuario	aquarium
el estanque	pond
el conejillo de Indias	guinea pig
el conejo	rabbit
el gato	cat
el hámster	hamster
el loro	parrot
el ratón	mouse
la tortuga	tortoise
coger; atrapar	to catch
dar de beber a	to give water to
dar de comer a	to feed
limpiar	to clean (out)
llevar de paseo a	to exercise
sacar a pasear a	to take for a walk

2 El nacimiento, el matrimonio y la muerte
Birth, marriage and death

¡FELIZ CUMPLEAÑOS!
HAPPY BIRTHDAY!

El alumbramiento Childbirth

el nacimiento	birth
el cumpleaños	birthday
la fecha de nacimiento	date of birth
el bebé	baby
el niño	boy
la niña	girl
la cesárea	caesarian
la comadrona	midwife
las contracciones	contractions
el embarazo	pregnancy
el feto	foetus
los fórceps	forceps
la matriz	womb

el/la médico	doctor
el parto	labour; delivery
el parto sin dolor	natural birth
varón/hembra	male / female
el bautismo	baptism
el bautizo	christening
la madrina	godmother
el nombre	name
el padrino	godfather
los padrinos	godparents
un regalo; un obsequio	present; gift

El bebé Baby

el bebé	baby
los padres	parents
la niñera	child minder
un-a canguro	baby sitter

¿Puedes darme . . . ?	Can I have the . . . ?
Dáme . . .	Pass me the . . .
Necesito . . .	I need the . . .
el andador	baby walker
el babero	bib
la bañera del bebé	baby's bath
el biberón	baby's bottle
la camiseta	vest
la canción de cuna	lullaby
la caja de música	musical chimes; music box
el chupete	dummy
el cochecito	pram
la comida para niños/potitos	baby food
la cuna	cot
el edredón	quilt
la manta	cot blanket
la sábana de cuna	cot sheet
el imperdible	nappy pin

2 El nacimiento, el matrimonio y la muerte
Birth, marriage and death

los juguetes	toys		
la leche	milk		
la leche en polvo	powdered milk		
la manopla	cloth		
el orinal	potty		
los pañales	nappies		
los pañales de usar y tirar; dodotis	disposable nappies		
el pijama	sleeping suit		
la sillita	push chair		
la sillita de coche	car seat		
el sonajero	rattle		
la toalla	towel		
las toallitas húmedas	wipes		
la trona	high chair		

nacer	to be born	destetar	to wean
el/ella nació . . .	he/she was born . . .	dormirse/	to get to sleep /
tener un bebé	to have a baby	despertarse	to wake up
Ella ha tenido		echar los	
un bebé.	She has had a baby.	dientes	to teethe
		eructar	to burp
alimentar	to feed	hervir/es-	
bañar	to bath	terilizar	to boil / sterilise
cambiar el		limpiar	to wipe
pañal	to change the	llorar	to cry
	nappy	mecer	to rock
crecer	to grow	sacar de paseo	to take for a walk
criar con		sonreír	to smile
biberón	to bottle feed		
dar el pecho a	to breast feed		

El/ella . . .	He/she . . .
llora mucho	cries a lot
no duerme	doesn't sleep
Necesito . . .	I need . . .
crema para . . .	cream for . . .
un culito escocido	a sore bottom
las quemaduras de sol	sunburn

2 El nacimiento, el matrimonio y la muerte
Birth, marriage and death

medicina para . . .	medicine for . . .
la indigestión	indigestion
la dentición	teething
la tos	a cough

¿Cuándo le toca una toma?	When should he/she be fed?
¿Cuándo le toca dormir?	When should he/she have a sleep?

¡OTRA VEZ!

● *Activity:* ¡Ayuda a Mamá! ¿Qué es lo que no encuentra?
Help mother! What can't she find?

2 El nacimiento, el matrimonio y la muerte
Birth, marriage and death

CRECIENDO
GROWING UP

el/la crío-a	*infant*
el/la pequeñito-a	*toddler*
el/la niño-a	*child*
el/la adolescente	*adolescent*
la pubertad	*puberty*
la bicicleta	*bicycle*
la caja de los juguetes	*toy box*
el cassette para niños	*children's cassette*
el coche de juguete	*toy car*
el cochecito	*push chair*
las construcciones	*building bricks*
los juegos de aprendizaje	*early learning games*
los juguetes	*toys*
el libro de cuentos para niños	*children's story book*

el rompecabezas	*jigsaw*
los trenes/coches en miniatura	*model trains / cars*
el triciclo	*tricycle*
el video para niños	*children's video*
¿Hay . . . ?	*Is there a . . . ?*
un columpio	*swing*
un parque infantil	*children's playground*
una rueda; un tiovivo	*roundabout*
un tobogán	*slide*
sentarse	*to sit up*
gatear	*to crawl*
caerse	*to fall*
aprender a andar	*to learn to walk*
aprender a hablar	*to learn to talk*
jugar	*to play*
crecer	*to grow up*

¿Es . . . ?	*Is it . . . ?*
seguro-a	*safe*
peligroso-a	*dangerous*
apropiado-a para niños de (3) años	*suitable for (3) year olds*

2 El nacimiento, el matrimonio y la muerte
Birth, marriage and death

EL AMOR Y EL MATRIMONIO
LOVE AND MARRIAGE

¡Te quiero!   *I love you!*

el amigo/novio	*boy friend*
la amiga/novia	*girl friend*
el compromiso	*engagement*
el/la prometido-a	*fiancé-e*
el cónyuge; la pareja	*partner*
la petición de mano	*proposal*
el/la amante	*lover*
el heterosexual	*heterosexual*
el homosexual; el gay	*homosexual*
la lesbiana	*lesbian*

quererse	*to love each other*
enamorarse	*to fall in love*
prometerse	*to get engaged*
salir juntos	*to go out together*
acostarse juntos	*to sleep together*
tener relaciones sexuales con...	*to have sex with...*

EL MATRIMONIO
MARRIAGE

¡Felicidades!
Congratulations!

EL ANILLO

el anillo	*ring*
el aniversario de boda	*wedding anniversary*
la boda	*wedding*
la boda civil	*civil marriage*
las bodas de plata/de oro	*silver / gold wedding*
la boda por la iglesia	*church wedding*
la ceremonia	*ceremony*
la dama de honor	*maid of honour*
el día de la boda	*wedding-day*
la invitación	*invitation*
la luna de miel	*honeymoon*
el marido	*husband*
la mujer; esposa	*wife*
la novia	*bride*
el novio	*bridegroom*
el padrino/ la madrino	*best man / matron of honour*
el paje	*page boy*
la partida de casamiento	*certificate*
los recién casados	*newly-weds*
el regalo de boda	*wedding present*
el registro civil	*registry office*
el traje de novia	*wedding dress*

EL ESTADO CIVIL
MARITAL STATUS

Soy...	*I am...*
soltero-a	*single*

Estoy...	*I am...*
casado-a	*married*
divorciado-a	*divorced*
separado-a	*separated*
viviendo con...	*living with...*

2 El nacimiento, el matrimonio y la muerte
Birth, marriage and death

el apellido de soltera	*maiden name*	el divorcio	*divorce*
el apellido de casada	*married name*	casarse	*to get married*
la separación	*separation*	separarse	*to get separated*
		divorciarse	*to get divorced*

LA MUERTE *DEATH*

Mi . . . ha muerto.	*My . . . has died.*
marido	*husband*
mujer	*wife*
amigo-a	*friend*
Estoy . . .	*I am (a) . . .*
desconsolado-a	*bereaved*
viuda	*widow*
viudo	*widower*

EL FUNERAL
The funeral

		dar un ataque al corazón	*to have a heart attack*
		dar el pésame	*to convey one's condolences*
el ataúd	*coffin*		
el cementerio	*cemetery*		
el duelo	*mourners*	enterrar	*to bury*
el entierro	*burial*	estar de luto	*to mourn*
la incineración	*cremation*	matarse	*to kill oneself*
el luto	*mourning*	morir en un accidente	*to be killed in an accident*
el testamento	*will*	ser envenenado	*to be poisoned*
la tumba	*grave*	suicidarse	*to commit suicide*
		tener cáncer	*to have cancer*
morirse	*to die*		
dar una apoplejía	*to have a stroke*	el/la heredero-a	*heir / heiress*
		heredar	*to inherit*

Deseo expresarle mi más sentido pésame.	*I would like to convey my condolences.*
Reciba mi más sincero pésame por tan dolorosa pérdida.	*I am very sorry to learn of your sad loss.*

3 La ropa y la moda *Clothes and fashion*

LA MODA
FASHION

la casa de modas	*fashion house*
el/la cliente	*client*
el/la comentarista	*commentator*
el desfile de modelos	*fashion show*
el/la diseñador-a	*designer*
el/la fotógrafo	*photographer*
el/la modelo	*model*
el modisto	*couturier*
la pasarela	*cat walk*
la revista de modas	*fashion magazine*

LA ROPA
CLOTHES

la bata; el batín	*dressing gown*
la blusa	*blouse*
los calcetines	*socks*
la camisa	*shirt*
la camisa polo	*polo shirt*
la camiseta	*T-shirt*
el camisón	*nightdress*
el chaleco	*waistcoat*
el chandal	*track suit*
el cinturón	*belt*
la corbata	*tie*
el delantal	*apron*
el esmoquin	*dinner jacket*
la falda	*skirt*
las medias	*stockings*
los pantalones	*trousers*
los pantalones cortos	*shorts*
los pantis	*tights*
el pijama	*pyjamas*
la rebeca	*cardigan*
la sudadera	*sweat shirt*

el suéter	*jumper*
el suéter de cuello cisne	*roll neck sweater*
los tirantes	*braces*
el traje	*suit*
el traje de noche	*evening dress*
el uniforme	*uniform*
los vaqueros; tejanos	*jeans*
el vestido	*dress*

La ropa interior *Underwear*

el body	*body*
las bragas	*knickers*
los calzoncillos	*underpants; briefs*
la camiseta	*vest*
la combinación	*slip*
la faja	*girdle*
el liguero	*suspender belt*
la media combinación	*underskirt*
el sujetador	*bra*

La ropa de abrigo *Outerwear*

el abrigo	*coat*
el anorak	*anorak*
la bufanda	*scarf*
la capucha	*hood*
la chaqueta	*jacket*
la gabardina	*rain coat*
la gorra	*cap*
la gorra de béisbol	*baseball cap*
el gorro de lana	*woolly hat*
los guantes	*gloves*
el impermeable	*mac*
el pañuelo de cabeza	*headscarf*
el paraguas	*umbrella*
el sombrero	*hat*

3 La ropa y la moda *Clothes and fashion*

La ropa de baño *Swimwear*

el bañador	*swimsuit*
el bikini	*bikini*
el gorro de baño	*swim hat*
el pantalón de baño	*trunks*
el traje de baño	*swimming costume*

EL CALZADO
FOOTWEAR

las aletas	*flippers*
las botas	*boots*
las botas de esquiar	*ski boots*
las botas de fútbol	*football boots*
las botas de goma	*rubber boots*

los cordones	*laces*
las sandalias	*sandals*
las zapatillas	*slippers*
las zapatillas de deporte	*trainers*
los zapatos	*shoes*
los zapatos con cordones	*lace-ups*
los zapatos de tacón alto	*high heeled shoes*

cambiarse	*to change*
llevar	*to wear*
ponerse	*to put on*
probarse	*to try . . . on*
quitarse	*to take off*
quitarse la ropa	*to get undressed*
vestirse	*to get dressed*

¡OTRA VEZ!

● Activity: ¿Qué llevan? *What are they wearing?*

(a)   (b)   (c)   (d)

57

PARTES DE LAS PRENDAS
PARTS OF THE GARMENTS

el bolsillo	*pocket*
la costura	*seam*
el cuello	*collar*
el cuerpo	*bodice*
el dobladillo	*hem*
el doblez	*turn-up*
la manga	*sleeve*
el ojal	*buttonhole*
el pliegue	*pleat*
el puño	*cuff*
la sisa	*dart*
la solapa	*lapel*

Tejidos *Materials*

de algodón	*cotton*
de encaje	*lace*
de fieltro	*felt*
de goma	*rubber*
de lana	*wool*
de lino	*linen*
de nilón	*nylon*
de plástico	*plastic*
de poliéster	*polyester*
de punto	*knitted*
de raso	*satin*
de seda	*silk*
de tela vaquera	*denim*
de terciopelo	*velvet*
de tweed	*tweed*

PIELES
FURS/LEATHER

de ante	*suede*
de charol	*patent leather*
de cuero	*leather*
de napa	*imitation leather*
de piel	*fur / leather*
de piel falsa	*artificial fur*
de visón	*mink*

LA COSTURA
SEWING

¡A coser!	*Sew it up!*
la aguja	*needle*
el alfiler	*pin*
el botón	*button*
el corchete	*fastener*
la cremallera	*zip*
el dedal	*thimble*
el hilo	*thread*
el imperdible	*safety pin*
la máquina de coser	*sewing machine*
el metro	*measuring tape*
el patrón	*pattern*
la puntada	*stitch*
las tijeras	*scissors*

ADJETIVOS ÚTILES
USEFUL ADJECTIVES

ajustado-a	*tight fitting*
ancho-a	*loose*
arrugado-a	*crumpled*
clásico-a	*classical*
con dibujo/liso-a	*patterned / plain*
confeccionado-a	*off-the-peg*
de cuadros	*checked*
de cuadros escoceses	*tartan*
elegante	*smart*
estampado-a	*printed*
estrecho-a	*tight*
de etiqueta	*formal*
de flores	*floral*
largo-a/corto-a	*long / short*
de lunares	*spotted*
de moda	*fashionable*

3 La ropa y la moda *Clothes and fashion*

muy holgado-a	*baggy*		la prensa para	
no combina bien	*ill-matching*		pantalones	*trouser press*
pasado-a			acortar	*to shorten*
de moda	*old fashioned*		alargar	*to lengthen*
plisado-a	*pleated*		arreglar	*to alter*
de rayas	*striped*		cambiar	*to change*
de sport	*casual*		colgar	*to hang up*
			coser	*to sew*

EL CUIDADO DE LA ROPA
CLOTHES CARE

			hacer	*to make*
la percha	*coat hanger*		limpiar	*to clean*
la percha			limpiar en seco	*to dry clean*
para faldas	*skirt hanger*		planchar	*to iron*
el perchero	*coatstand*		rasgarse	*to tear*
la plancha	*iron*		teñir	*to stain*
la plancha			unir	*to tie*
de vapor	*steam iron*		zurcir	*to mend*

¡OTRA VEZ!

● Activity: ¿Qué están poniendo en la maleta? *What are they packing?*

¿Lavar o limpiar en seco?	*Wash or dry clean?*
Símbolos de lavado	*Washing symbols*
Limpieza en seco; lavar en seco	*Dry clean only*
Lavado a mano	*Handwash only*
Lavar aparte	*Wash separately*
Usar agua templada (30°C)	*Use tepid water (30°C)*
No usar secadora	*Do not tumble dry*
No usar lejía	*Do not use bleach*
No planchar	*Do not iron*
Planchado a temperatura media	*Use only cool iron*
Extender húmedo	*Spread out to dry*
No mantener en remojo	*Do not soak*
No usar detergente	*Do not use detergent*
Usar jabón neutro	*Use neutral soap*
Limpiar con trapo húmedo	*Wipe with a damp cloth*
Puede usar secadora	*Can be tumble dried*
Aclarar sin retorcer	*Rinse without wringing*

COMPLEMENTOS
ACCESSORIES

el bolso de bandolera	*shoulder bag*
el bolso de mano	*handbag*
el chal	*shawl*
el cinturón	*belt*
los guantes	*gloves*
el monedero	*purse*
el pañuelo	*scarf*
el paraguas	*umbrella*
el reloj (de pulsera)	*watch*

JOYAS Y PERFUMES
JEWELLERY AND PERFUME

el alfiler de corbata	*tie pin*
el anillo	*ring*
la alianza	*wedding ring*
el anillo de compromiso	*engagement ring*
el anillo de sello	*signet ring*
la bisutería	*costume jewellery*
el broche	*brooch*
el colgante	*pendant*
el collar	*necklace*
la cruz	*cross*
la diadema	*tiara*
los gemelos	*cuff links*
los pendientes	*earrings*
la pulsera	*bracelet*

Metales y piedras preciosas y semi-preciosas
Metals and precious and semi-precious stones

¡Un brillante es para siempre!
Diamonds are forever.

la amatista	*amethyst*
el bronce	*bronze*

3 La ropa y la moda *Clothes and fashion*

el cobre	copper	el zafiro	sapphire
el coral	coral		
el cristal	crystal	el quilate	carat
el diamante;		la talla	cut
el brillante	diamond		
el esmalte	enamel		

Perfumes *Perfume*

la esmeralda	emerald		
el lapislázuli	lapis lazuli	el agua de	toilet water;
el ópalo	opal	colonia	eau de cologne
el oro	gold	de flores	flowery
la perla	pearl	la fragancia	scent
la plata	silver	de lavanda	lavender
el platino	platinum	el vaporizador	spray
el rubí	ruby		

¡OTRA VEZ!

● *Activity:* ¿Qué van a comprar? *What are they going to buy?*

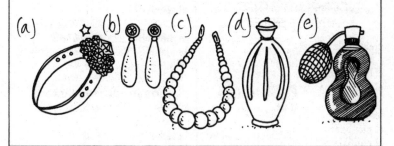

(a) (b) (c) (d) (e)

COMPUESTOS DE LOS ALIMENTOS:
INGREDIENTES Y PREPARACIÓN
FOODSTUFFS AND FOOD PREPARATION

las calorías	*calories*	la harina	*flour*
el carbohidrato	*carbohydrate*	la harina	
la fibra	*fibre*	de maíz	*cornflour*
la grasa	*fat*	la harina	
los minerales	*minerals*	integral	*wholemeal flour*
las proteínas	*proteins*	la levadura	*yeast*
las vitaminas	*vitamins*	la sal fina	*fine salt*
		la sal gorda	*coarse salt*
integral	*wholemeal*	la sal marina	*sea salt*
mono-			
insaturado-a	*monounsaturated*		

Las grasas *Fat*

orgánico-a	*organic*		
poliinsaturado-a	*polyunsaturated*	el aceite	*oil*
		el aceite de	
Sin colorantes ni	*No artificial*	oliva	*olive oil*
conservantes	*colouring or*	el aceite de	
	preservatives	girasol	*sunflower oil*
		la manteca	*animal fat*
líquido-a	*liquid*	la mantequilla	*butter*
sólido-a	*solid*	la margarina	*margarine*

Los productos lácteos
Dairy goods

¡(No) es sano!	*It's good/bad for you!*		
		la leche	*milk*
la cocina	*cooking* (la cuisine)	la mantequilla	*butter*
la cocinera	*cook*	la nata	*cream*
la gastronomía	*gastronomy*	el queso	*cheese*
el jefe de cocina	*chef*	cabrales	*de cabrales (Spanish blue cheese)*
la receta	*recipe*		

LOS INGREDIENTES
COOKING INGREDIENTS

		de bola	*Edam type cheese*
el azúcar	*sugar*	manchego	*manchego (ewe's milk cheese)*
el azúcar		el yogur	*yoghurt*
morena	*brown sugar*		
el bicarbonato		semi-descremado-a	
sódico	*bicarbonate of soda*		*half fat*

4 La comida y la bebida *Food and drink*

El huevo *Egg*

la yema	*egg yolk*
la clara del huevo	*egg white*

Los frutos secos
Dried fruit and nuts

la almendra	*almond*
la avellana	*hazelnut*
el cacahuete	*peanut*
el coco	*coconut*
el dátil	*date*
el higo	*fig*
la nuez	*walnut*
la pasa	*raisin; sultana*
la pipa	*sunflower seed*
el pistacho	*pistachio*

Las legumbres *Pulses*

las alubias blancas	*butter beans*
las alubias pintas	*red kidney beans*
los garbanzos	*chick peas*
las lentejas	*lentils*
el arroz	*rice*
los espaguetis	*spaghetti*
la pasta	*pasta*

Los utensilios de cocina
Cooking utensils

el abrebotellas	*bottle opener*
el abrelatas	*tin opener*
el afilador de cuchillos	*knife sharpener*
la bandeja de horno	*baking tray*
el batidor	*whisk*
el cazo	*saucepan*
el colador	*sieve*
la cuchara de madera	*wooden spoon*
el cuchillo de cocina	*kitchen knife*
el cuenco	*bowl*
el escurridor	*colander*
los guantes para el horno	*oven gloves*
el minipimer	*hand held food processor*
el molde desmontable para pastel	*cake tin*
el molinillo de café	*coffee grinder*
la parrilla	*griddle*
el peso	*weighing scales*
el rodillo	*rolling pin*
el sacacorchos	*corkscrew*
la sartén	*frying pan*
la tabla de picar	*chopping board*
las tijeras	*scissors*
el ajuste	*setting*
el avisador	*timer*
la batidora	*mixer*
la cafetera	*coffee machine*
el grill	*grill*
el quemador	*hob*
el termostato	*thermostat*
el tostador	*toaster*

Las hierbas y las especias
Herbs and spices

Las hierbas aromáticas	**Herbs**
la albahaca	*basil*
el anís	*aniseed*
el azafrán	*saffron*
el eneldo	*dill*
el estragón	*tarragon*
la hierbabuena	*mint*
el laurel	*bayleaves*

4 La comida y la bebida *Food and drink*

el orégano	oregano	el jengibre	ginger
el perejil	parsley	la nuez moscada	nutmeg
el romero	rosemary	el pimentón	paprika
la salvia	sage	la pimienta	pepper
el tomillo	thyme		
		el ajo	garlic
Las especias	**Spices**	el edulcorante	artificial sweetener
la canela	cinnamon	la miel	honey
el clavo	clove	la mostaza	mustard
el comino	cumin	la vainilla	vanilla

LOS SABORES   TASTE AND FLAVOUR

Mmm . . . ¡Me gusta!	Mmmmm . . . I like it!
¡Está riquísimo!	It's delicious!
¡No me gusta! ¡Está . . .!	I don't like it. It's . . .!

agrio-a	sour	incomible	inedible
ahumado-a	smoked	insípido-a	tasteless
amargo-a	bitter	sabroso-a	tasty
delicioso-a;		salado-a	salted
rico-a	delicious	seco-a	dried
dulce	sweet	soso-a	bland; lacking salt
duro-a	tough; stale (bread)	tierno-a	tender

VERBOS ÚTILES
USEFUL VERBS

		gratinar	to cook au gratin
		guisar	to stew
		hervir	to boil
asar	to bake; roast	hornear	to roast
asar a la parrilla	to grill	lavar	to wash
batir	to beat	limpiar	to clean
brasear	to braise	mezclar	to mix
calentar	to heat	pelar	to peel
cocer	to cook	picar	to chop; mince
cocer al vapor	to steam	pringar	to baste
colar	to strain	rellenar	to stuff; fill
cortar	to cut	remover	to stir
derretir	to melt	sazonar	to season
enfriar	to cool	secar	to dry
estofar	to stew	tostar	to toast
freír	to fry	triturar	to grind; crush

4 La comida y la bebida *Food and drink*

FRUTA Y VERDURA *FRUIT AND VEGETABLES*

¡Alimentación sana, natural y equilibrada!	*Healthy Eating! Vitamins! Fibre!*

La fruta *Fruit*

		el mango	*mango*
		la manzana	*apple*
la compota		el melocotón	*peach*
de fruta	*fruit purée*	el melón	*melon*
la macedonia		el membrillo	*quince*
de frutas	*fruit salad*	la mora	*blackberry*
la mermelada	*jam*	la naranja	*orange*
		el níspero	*medlar*
el aguacate	*avocado*	la pera	*pear*
el albaricoque	*apricot*	la piña	*pineapple*
la cereza	*cherry*	el plátano	*banana*
la chirimoya	*custard apple*	el pomelo	*grapefruit*
la ciruela	*plum*	la sandía	*watermelon*
la frambuesa	*raspberry*	las uvas	*grapes*
la fresa	*strawberry*		
la granada	*pomegranite*		
el higo	*fig*	pelar	*to peel*
el kiwi	*kiwi*	la piel	*skin*
la lima	*lime*	las pipas	*pips*
el limón	*lemon*	las semillas	*seeds*
la mandarina	*mandarin orange*	trocear	*to cut up*

Las verduras *Vegetables*

¡Lavar bien antes de consumirlas!	*Wash before eating!*

cocido-a	*cooked*	el brécol	*broccoli*
crudo-a	*raw*	el calabacín	*courgette*
rallado-a	*grated*	la cebolla	*onion*
		el champiñón;	
la aceituna	*olive*	la seta	*mushroom*
la alcachofa	*artichoke*	la col; el repollo	*cabbage*
el ajo	*garlic*	la col de	
el apio	*celery*	Bruselas	*Brussel sprouts*
la berenjena	*aubergine*	la col roja	*red cabbage*

4 La comida y la bebida *Food and drink*

la coliflor	*cauliflower*	la patata	*potato*
los guisantes	*peas*	el pimiento	*pepper*
los espárragos	*asparagus*	el puerro	*leek*
las espinacas	*spinach*	la remolacha	*beetroot*
las habas	*broad beans*	la zanahoria	*carrot*
la habichuela	*runner bean*		
la judía verde	*green bean*	la lechuga	*lettuce*
el nabo	*turnip*	el pepino	*cucumber*
		el tomate	*tomato*

4 La comida y la bebida *Food and drink*

LAS BEBIDAS
DRINKS

Las bebidas calientes
Hot drinks

una taza de ...	*a cup of ...*
con leche	*with milk*
con limón	*with lemon*
con nata	*with cream*
el azúcar	*sugar*
el edulcorante	*sweetener*
la cucharilla	*teaspoon*
el platillo	*saucer*

El té	**Tea**
la bolsa de té	*tea-bag*
la manzanilla	*camomile tea*
la tisana	*tisane*

El café	**Coffee**
el café con leche	*white coffee*
el café instantáneo	*instant coffee*
el café solo	*black coffee*
el cortado	*small coffee with a little milk*
el descafeinado	*decaffeinated coffee*
el chocolate caliente	*hot chocolate*

Los refrescos *Cold drinks*

una botella	*a bottle*
un brik	*a carton*
una lata	*a can*
un vaso	*a glass*
el agua	*water*
el agua mineral sin gas	*still mineral water*
el agua mineral con gas	*carbonated mineral water*
el batido (de fresa)	*milk shake (strawberry)*
la coca-cola	*coca cola*
la granizada (de limón)	*iced drink (lemon)*
la horchata	*tiger nut milk*
un refresco de limón	*lemonade*
un refresco de naranja	*orangeade*
la tónica	*tonic*
un zumo	*fruit juice*
de manzana	*apple*
de naranja	*orange*
de tomate	*tomato*

¡Salud! *Cheers!*

El alcohol	**Alcohol**
la cerveza	*beer (lager)*
la cerveza negra	*dark beer (stout)*
la cerveza sin alcohol	*alcohol free beer*
el vino ...	*... wine*
tinto	*red*
blanco	*white*
rosado	*rosé*
el cava	*cava (Spanish sparkling wine)*
el champán	*champagne*
el fino	*dry sherry*
la manzanilla	*manzanilla*
el vino de mesa	*table wine*
el vino dulce/seco	*sweet / dry wine*
el coñac	*brandy; cognac*
el ron	*rum*
la sangría	*sangria*
el whisky	*whisky*
el vodka	*vodka*
el cubata	*rum and coke*

4 La comida y la bebida *Food and drink*

el tinto de verano	*red wine and carbonated water*	con/sin hielo	*with / without ice*
		beber; tomar	*to drink*
con/sin limón	*with / without lemon*	sorber	*to sip*

¡OTRA VEZ!

● Activity: What would you say to order these drinks?

Quisiera . . .   *I would like . . .*

4 La comida y la bebida *Food and drink*

LAS COMIDAS
MEALS

¡Que aproveche!
Enjoy your meal!

el almuerzo	*lunch*
la cena	*dinner; supper*
el desayuno	*breakfast*
la merienda	*tea; afternoon snack*
la tapa	*tapa; small snack*

El desayuno *Breakfast*

los cereales	*cereal*
las galletas	*biscuits*
la mantequilla	*butter*
la margarina	*margarine*
la mermelada	*jam*
la miel	*honey*
la nata	*cream*
el pomelo	*grapefruit*
una tostada	*a piece of toast*
el zumo de naranja	*orange juice*

El almuerzo y la cena *Lunch and dinner*

las patatas . . .	*. . . potatoes*
al horno	*baked*
asadas	*roast*
cocidas	*boiled*
fritas	*chips*
el puré de patatas	*creamed potatoes*
las verduras . . .	*. . . vegetables*
(See also: *Fruit and vegetables*, page 65.)	
cocidas	*cooked*
crudas	*raw*
hervidas	*boiled*
rehogadas	*sautéed*
los huevos . . .	*. . . eggs*
duros	*hard boiled*
fritos	*fried*
pasados por agua	*soft boiled*
revueltos	*scrambled*
la tortilla	*omelette*
la tortilla de patatas	*potato omelette*
la tortilla francesa	*plain omelette*

LA COMIDA
FOOD

La carne *Meat*

el cerdo	*pork*
el cordero	*lamb*
la ternera	*beef*
la ternera de Ávila	*veal*
la carne picada	*minced meat*
la salchicha	*sausage*

Las aves *Poultry*

la oca	*goose*
el pato	*duck*
el pavo	*turkey*
el pollo	*chicken*

La caza *Game*

el conejo	*rabbit*
la cordoniz	*quail*
el faisán	*pheasant*
la liebre	*hare*
la perdiz	*partridge*
el venado	*venison*

Los fiambres
Cooked meat; charcuterie

el beicon	*bacon*
el chorizo	*chorizo*
el foie-gras	*paté*
el jamón de York	*boiled ham*
el jamón serrano	*raw ham*
el salami	*salami*
el salchichón	*salami-type sausage*
la costilla	*rib*

la chuleta	*chop*
el filete	*steak*
la pierna	*leg*
el pescado	*fish*
(See also page 112)	
el pescado ahumado	*smoked fish*

El pan *Bread*

la barra	*baguette*
el croissant	*croissant*
las galletas saladas	*crackers*
el pan integral	*wholemeal bread*
el pan rallado	*breadcrumbs*
el panecillo/ la viena	*bread roll*
el bocadillo	*sandwich (roll)*
el sándwich; el emparedado	*sandwich (English typ*

No tomo carne/ productos lácteos.	*I don't eat meat / dairy products.*
Soy vegetariano-a.	*I am a vegetarian.*
Me encanta ...	*I love ...*
Mi ... favorito-a es ...	*My favourite ... is ...*

PONER LA MESA
LAYING THE TABLE

la cuchara	*spoon*
el cuchillo	*knife*
el mantel	*tablecloth*
la servilleta	*napkin*
el tenedor	*fork*
el salvamanteles	*place mat*
la copa	*glass (for sherry, champagne, etc.)*

4 La comida y la bebida *Food and drink*

el cuenco	*bowl*		
la jarra	*jug*		
el platillo	*saucer*		
el plato	*plate; dish*		
la taza	*cup*		
el vaso	*glass* (for milk, water etc.)		

Los condimentos
Condiments

el aceite	*oil*
la mostaza	*mustard*
la pimienta	*pepper*
la sal	*salt*
el vinagre	*vinegar*
el kétchup	*tomato sauce*
la mayonesa	*mayonnaise*

EXPRESIONES ÚTILES
USEFUL EXPRESSIONS

Está en . . .	*It's in / on . . .*
el cajón	*the drawer*
el armarito	*the wallcupboard*
la nevera	*the fridge*
el lavavajillas	*the dishwasher*
la repisa	*the shelf*
¡Que aproveche!	*Enjoy your meal!* (Bon appétit!)
¡Igualmente!	*And you too!*
Me gusta . . .	*I like . . .*
No me gusta . . .	*I don't like . . .*
No puedo más.	*I'm full.*
Es demasiado.	*It's too much.*
Está . . .	*It's . . .*
soso-a	*bland; lacking salt*
demasiado agrio-a	*too sour*
demasiado caliente	*too hot*
demasiado dulce	*too sweet*
demasiado frío-a	*too cold*

4 La comida y la bebida *Food and drink*

COMER FUERA DE CASA
EATING OUT

¡Oiga, por favor!
Excuse me, please!

el bar	*bar*
el café	*café*
el comedor	*dining room; canteen*
la hamburguesería	*fast food restaurant*
la marisquería	*seafood bar / restaurant*
la pizzería	*pizzeria*
el restaurante	*restaurant*
el self service	*self-service*
la venta	*country inn*
el cenicero	*ashtray*
el cubierto	*place setting*
los cubiertos	*cutlery*
la mesa	*table*
el palillo	*tooth pick*
la salsa	*sauce*
la servilleta	*serviette*
la silla	*chair*

el camarero	*waiter*
la camarera	*waitress*
el sumiller	*wine waiter*
la cuenta	*bill*
el IVA	*VAT*
la propina	*tip*
el recibo	*receipt*
el servicio	*service charge*
la vuelta	*change*
la carta	*menu*
el menú del día	*menu of the day*
el primer plato	*first course*
los entremeses	*hors d'oeuvre*
la ensalada	*salad*
el plato principal	*main course*
el segundo plato	*second course*
el plato de pescado	*fish course*
el postre	*dessert*
el queso	*cheese*
la fruta	*fruit*
beber	*to drink*
comer	*to eat*
pagar	*to pay*
tomar	*to have* (food/drink)

Las tapas *Tapas*

Una tapa de ...	A tapa of ...
aceitunas	*olives*
bacalao con tomate	*cod in tomato sauce*
carne en salsa	*meat in sauce*
champiñón al ajillo	*mushrooms in garlic*
ensaladilla rusa	*potato & vegetable salad*
gambas	*prawns*
jamón	*raw ham*
queso	*cheese*
tortilla	*potato omelette*

4 La comida y la bebida *Food and drink*

Platos típicos
Typical dishes

el cocido	*chickpea and meat stew (Castilla)*
la fabada	*bean and pork stew (Asturias)*
el gazpacho	*cold tomato soup (Andalucía)*
la paella	*paella (Valencia)*

Aquí se come bien	*Here you eat well*
muy bien	*very well*
estupendamente	*very very well*
¡demasiado!	*too much!*
¿Me/nos trae la cuenta, por favor?	*Can I have the bill please?*
¿Podemos pagar por separado, por favor?	*Can we pay separately please?*
¿Está incluido el servicio?	*Is service included?*
¿Tengo que dejar propina?	*Should I leave a tip?*
¿Cuánto?	*How much?*
¡Para el bote!	*(said on giving a tip)*

¡OTRA VEZ!

● *Activity:* Dígale al camarero qué va a tomar. *Tell the waiter what you would like:*

de primero . . .	*as a starter*
de segundo . . .	*as main course*
de postre . . .	*for dessert*
para beber . . .	*to drink*

LA CASA Y LA VIVIENDA
HOUSING AND ACCOMMODATION

la casa . . .	*. . . house*
adosada	*terraced*
semi-adosada	*semi-detached*
unifamiliar	*detached*
la casa de campo	*cottage*
el chalet	*chalet*
la granja; el cortijo	*farm*
la villa	*villa*
la vivienda de protección oficial	*council house / flat*
una casa con . . .	*a house with . . .*
garaje	*a garage*
jardín	*a garden*
piscina	*a swimming pool*
plaza de aparcamiento	*a parking space*
el piso	*flat*
la casa/el piso alquilado-a	*rented house / flat*
la comunidad de propietarios	*owners' association*
el ascensor	*lift*
el portero electrónico	*answering device*
Soy/somos propietario(-s) de	
mi/nuestra vivienda.	*I / we own our own house.*

5 La casa, el hogar y el jardín *House, home and garden*

la agencia inmobiliaria	*estate agency*
el agente inmobiliario	*agent*
el/la comprador-a	*buyer*
la escritura	*deeds*
la hipoteca	*mortgage*
la llave	*key*
el préstamo	*loan*
la sociedad de préstamo inmobiliario	*building society*

la valoración	*valuation*
el/la vendedor-a	*seller*
el ático	*attic flat*
el barrio	*district; quarter*
el bloque de pisos	*block of flats*
el centro	*town / city centre*
el duplex	*split-level flat*
el/la inquilino-a	*tenant*
la urbanización	*housing estate*
el anuncio	*advertisement*

VENDO piso, zona Reina Mercedes, todo exterior, cinco dormitorios, 3 baños, aire acondicionado, estupendo estado, recién reformado, precio interesante. Telf. 95-4356562/91-3597091.

TRIANA (Los Remedios), 3 dormitorios, 6.500.000 contado. Teléfono 4340590.

SANTA Clara, ocasión, Nuevo Continente, 4 dormitorios, cocina con gran office, 2 cuartos de baño, 1 aseo, aparcamiento propio, club social, 18.500.000 pesetas. 4676458.

MADRID, San Bernardo 83. Particular. Exterior, lujo, amueblado, climatizado. 17.000.000. 96-5126165, tardes.

SIMON Verde, próxima construcción, dos últimos pareados, 607 m^2 parcela, 240 m^2 construidos. Aruncy. 4275067.

OCASION, Valencina, dos últimos chalets independientes, cuatro dormitorios, 400 m^2 parcela, 14.500.000. Aruncy. 4275067.

OPORTUNIDAD. Residencial Helios. Por traslado vendo casa. 4239503.

SANTA Eufemia, adosado, 5 minutos Sevilla, 3 dormitorios, uno doble, salón chimenea, 2 baños, 1 aseo, armarios empotrados, jardín privado, garaje 2 plazas, solárium, piscina común. Urge por traslado. Ocasión, 10.500.000, más 3.300.000 hipoteca. 4152637.

cerca de . . .	*near to . . .*
situado-a en el campo	*rural situation*
tranquilo-a	*quiet*
en el centro	*central location*
el aire acondicionado	*air conditioning*
el aislamiento	*insulation*
la calefacción central	*central heating*
el doble acristalamiento	*double glazing*
la insonorización	*sound proofing*

el carbón	*coal*
el combustible sólido	*solid fuel*
la electricidad	*electricity*
el gas	*gas*
la madera	*wood*
el petróleo	*oil*
alquilar	*to rent; let*
compartir	*to share*
comprar	*to buy*
pagar	*to pay*
tomar prestado	*to borrow*

5 La casa, el hogar y el jardín *House, home and garden*

Las partes de la casa
Parts of the house

el garaje	*garage*
la pared	*wall*
la persiana	*shutter*
la puerta	*door*
la puerta	
principal	*front door*
la reja	*window bars*
el suelo	*floor*
el techo	*ceiling*
el tejado	*roof*
la ventana	*window*
la verja	*gate*
la azotea	*terrace*
el bajo	*ground floor*
el balcón;	
la terraza	*balcony*
el desván	*attic; loft*
las escaleras	*stairs*
el patio	*patio*
el primer piso	*first floor*
el sótano	*basement; cellar*

Las habitaciones *Rooms*

la cocina	*kitchen*
el comedor	*dining room*
el cuarto	
de baño	*bathroom*
el cuarto de	
los niños	*play room*
el descansillo	*landing*
el dormitorio	*bedroom*
el estudio	*study*
la habitación	*spare room;*
de invitados	*guest room*
el lavadero	*laundry room*
el salón; la sala	
de estar	*lounge; sitting room*
el trastero	*boxroom*
el vestíbulo	*entrance hall*

¡OTRA VEZ!

● *Label each room in this flat.*

76

LOS MUEBLES Y LOS OBJETOS DE LA CASA
FURNITURE AND FURNISHINGS

la alfombra	*rug*	la lavadora	*washing machine*
la almohada	*pillow*	el lavavajillas	*dishwasher*
el armario	*wardrobe*	la librería	*bookcase*
el armario		la maceta	*plant pot*
empotrado	*fitted wardrobe*	la manta	*blanket*
el armarito	*wall cupboard*	el mantel	*tablecloth*
el aseo	*toilet*	la mecedora	*rocking chair*
el azulejo	*wall tile*	la mesa	*table*
la baldosa	*floor tile*	la mesa de café	*coffee table*
la bañera	*bath*	la mesita	
la cama	*bed*	de noche	*bedside table*
el cenicero	*ashtray*	el microondas	*microwave*
la clavija	*plug*	el módulo	
la cocina	*cooker*	de cocina	*kitchen unit*
el cojín	*cushion*	la moqueta	*carpet*
la colcha	*bedspread*	el ordenador	
el colchón	*mattress*	personal	*personal computer*
la cómoda	*chest of drawers*	el papel pintado	*wallpaper*
las cortinas	*curtains*	la plancha	*iron*
la cristalería	*glassware*	el quemador	*hob*
el cuadro	*picture; painting*	el radiador	*radiator*
la cubertería	*cutlery*	la radio	*radio*
la cuna	*cot*	el reloj de pared	*clock*
el edredón	*quilt; duvet*	la sábana	*sheet*
el enchufe	*socket*	la secadora	*tumble drier*
el equipo		la servilleta	*towel*
de música	*stereo*	la silla	*chair*
el espejo	*mirror*	el sillón	*armchair*
la estantería	*shelves*	el sofá	*sofa*
el florero	*vase*	el sofá cama	*sofa bed*
el fregadero	*sink*	la tabla	
el frigorífico	*fridge*	de planchar	*ironing board*
el grifo del agua		el taburete	*stool*
caliente/fría	*hot / cold water tap*	el televisor	*television*
el horno	*oven*	la toalla	*towel*
el interruptor	*switch*	el tostador	*toaster*
la lámpara	*lamp*	la trona	*high chair*
la lámpara		la vajilla	*crockery*
de pie	*standard lamp*	el vídeo	*video recorder*
el lavabo	*washbasin*	el visillo	*net curtain*

5 La casa, el hogar y el jardín *House, home and garden*

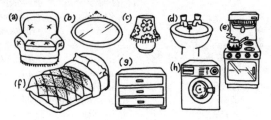
LAS TAREAS DE LA CASA   *HOUSEWORK*

Mi marido no trabaja.
Es amo de casa.

My husband doesn't work. He's a house husband.

la aspiradora	*vacuum cleaner*	el detergente	*detergent*
el cepillo;		la fregona	*mop*
la escoba	*brush*	la gamuza	*duster*
la cera para		el limpiacristales	*window cleaner*
muebles	*furniture polish*		*(detergent)*
el cubo	*bucket*	el limpiahornos	*oven cleaner*
el desinfectante	*disinfectant*	el papel	
		higiénico	*toilet paper*

el producto de limpieza para . . .
  el cuarto de baño   *bathroom cleaner*
  moquetas   *carpet cleaner*
  suelos   *floor cleaner*

78

el recogedor	*dustpan*
la toalla de papel para la cocina	*kitchen roll*
el trapo	*cloth*
la limpiadora; la asistenta	*cleaner (person)*
barrer	*to sweep*
cargar/vaciar el lavavajillas	*to load / unload the dishwasher*
fregar los platos	*to do the washing up*
hacer las camas	*to make the beds*
lavar la ropa	*to do the washing / laundry*
limpiar	*to clean*
limpiar el polvo	*to dust*
limpiar las ventanas	*to clean the windows*
pasar la aspiradora	*to put the sweeper over*
planchar	*to do the ironing*
poner la mesa	*to lay the table*
sacar brillo	*to polish*
secar los platos	*to wipe (plates)*

EL JARDÍN *GARDEN*

la horticultura	*horticulture*
la jardinería	*gardening*
el abono	*manure*
el árbol	*tree*
el arbusto	*bush; shrub*
el arriate	*flower bed*
los bulbos	*bulbs*
el camino	*path*
el césped	*lawn*
el fertilizante	*fertiliser*

Las flores *Flowers*

el clavel	*carnation*
el crisantemo	*chrysanthemum*
el geranio	*geranium*
el girasol	*sunflower*
el lirio	*lily*
la margarita	*daisy*
la rosa	*rose*
la hierba	*grass*
las hierbas	*herbs*
la huerta	*vegetable garden*
el invernadero	*greenhouse*
la maceta	*plant pot*
la planta	*plant*
las semillas	*seeds*

Los útiles de jardinería *Garden tools*

el aspersor	*sprinkler*
la azada	*hoe*
la carretilla	*wheelbarrow*
el cortacésped	*lawn mower*
el desplantador	*trowel*
la horquilla	*fork*
la manguera	*hose-pipe*
la pala	*spade*
el rastrillo	*rake*
la regadera	*watering can*
la sierra	*saw*
la sierra de cadena	*chain saw*
las tijeras de podar	*secateurs*
las tijeras de jardín	*shears*

5 La casa, el hogar y el jardín *House, home and garden*

Los muebles de jardín
Garden furniture

la barbacoa	*barbecue*
el bebedero para pájaros	*bird bath*
el cobertizo	*garden shed*
el columpio	*swing*
la hamaca	*hammock*
la mesa de jardín	*garden table*
la piscina para niños	*paddling pool*
la silla de jardín	*garden chair*
la sombrilla	*sunshade*
el tobogán	*slide*
el toldo	*awning*
la tumbona	*deckchair*
al sol	*in the sun*
a la sombra	*in the shade*

El árbol *Tree*

la hoja	*leaf*
la raíz	*root*
la rama	*branch*
la ramita	*twig*
el tronco	*trunk*
los árboles frutales	*fruit trees*
la semilla	*seed*
la plántula	*seedling*
la hoja	*leaf*
la planta	*plant*
la flor	*flower*
en flor	*in blossom*
el fruto	*fruit*
abonar	*to fertilise*
cavar	*to dig*
coger	*to pick*
cortar la hierba/ el césped	*to cut the grass / the lawn*
cultivar	*to cultivate; grow*
desherbar	*to weed*
plantar	*to plant*
podar	*to prune*
regar	*to water; irrigate*
sembrar	*to sow*

LAS PROFESIONES Y LOS EMPLEOS
JOBS

Soy . . .	*I am a / an . . .*
El/ella es . . .	*He / she is a / an . . .*
abogado	*lawyer*
actor/actriz	*actor / actress*
agricultor	*farmer*
artista	*artist*
bibliotecario-a	*librarian*
bombero	*fireman*
camarero-a	*waitress / waitress*
cantante	*singer*
carnicero-a	*butcher*
cartero	*postman*
cirujano	*surgeon*
cocinero-a	*cook*
comprador-a; encargado-a de compras	*buyer*
conductor-a	*driver*
conductor de camiones; camionero	*lorry driver*
contable	*accountant*
contratista	*builder*
dentista	*dentist*
dependiente	*shop assistant*
director-a de empresa	*company director*
diseñador-a de modas	*fashion designer*
diseñador-a gráfico	*graphic designer*
diseñador-a industrial	*industrial designer*
electricista	*electrician*
empleado-a de banco	*bank employee*
enfermera	*nurse*
estudiante	*student*
farmacéutico-a	*chemist*
fisioterapeuta	*physiotherapist*
fontanero	*plumber*
funcionario-a (del estado)	*civil servant*
gerente	*manager*
guía de turismo	*tour guide*
hombre/mujer de negocios	*businessman / woman*
ingeniero	*engineer*
intérprete	*interpreter*
jardinero	*gardener*
limpiador-a	*cleaner*
marinero	*sailor*
mecánico	*mechanic*
médico	*doctor*
notario	*solicitor*
oficinista	*clerk*
operador-a de ordenadores	*computer operator*
panadero	*baker*
peluquero-a	*hairdresser*
periodista	*journalist*
pintor decorador	*painter and decorator*
policía	*policeman*
profesor-a	*teacher*
profesor-a de universidad	*lecturer*
químico (industrial)	*chemist*
radiógrafo	*radiographer*
recepcionista	*receptionist*
repartidor-a	*delivery man / woman*
representante; viajante	*sales representative*
secretario-a	*secretary*
soldado	*soldier*
taxista	*taxi driver*
telefonista	*telephonist*
traductor-a	*translator*
vendedor-a; encargado-a de ventas	*salesman / woman*

Trabajo...	*I work...*
a tiempo parcial	*part-time*
como freelance	*freelance*
Soy autónomo-a.	*I am self-employed.*
Estoy desempleado-a/en paro.	*I am unemployed.*
el curso de reciclaje	*re-training course*
la oficina de empleo	*employment office*
el subsidio de desempleo	*unemployment benefit*

LOS SINDICATOS
UNIONS

el acuerdo	*agreement*
el/la afiliado-a	*trades union member*
la cuota de afiliado	*membership fee*
el/la delegado-a	*delegate*
el/la dirigente sindical	*trades union official*
el/la enlace sindical	*shop steward*
la huelga	*strike*
la huelga de celo	*work to rule*
la reunión sindical	*trades union meeting*
el sindicato	*trade union*
la tarjeta de afiliado; el carnet	*membership card*

EL SUELDO   PAY

el día de paga	*pay day*
la hoja de sueldo; la nómina	*pay slip*
los ingresos; el sueldo	*earnings*
el impuesto sobre la renta	*income tax*
el IVA	*VAT*

el jornal	*wage*
el plan de pensiones	*pension plan*
las retenciones	*deductions*
la retención fiscal	*P.A.Y.E.*
el salario	*salary*
el seguro social	*National Insurance*
el sobre de paga	*pay packet*
la transferencia bancaria	*bank transfer*
semanal	*weekly*
mensual	*monthly*
neto	*net*
bruto	*gross*
asistir a una reunión	*to attend a meeting*
comprar	*to buy*
discutir	*to discuss*
(no) estar de acuerdo	*to agree / disagree*
ganar	*to earn*
fichar a la llegada/ a la salida	*to clock on / off*
hacer horas extraordinarias	*to do overtime*
tener reuniones	*to have meetings*

6 El mundo del trabajo *Jobs and work*

trabajar	*to work*	vender	*to sell*
trabajar por		viajar	*to travel*
turnos	*to work shifts*		

EL LUGAR DE TRABAJO *THE WORKPLACE*

Trabajo en...	*I work in a/an...*
El/ella trabaja en...	*He/she works in a/an*
un almacén	*warehouse*
un ambulatorio	*surgery*
una cadena de montaje	*assembly line*
casa	*at home*
una clínica	*clinic*
un colegio	*school*
el control de calidad	*quality control*
el embalaje	*packaging*
una empresa	*company*
un estudio	*studio*
una fábrica	*factory*
un hospital	*hospital*
un hotel	*hotel*
los negocios	*business*
una oficina	*office*
la oficina central	*head office*
la producción	*production*
un punto de venta al por menor	*retail outlet*
el reparto; la entrega	*delivery*
un restaurante	*restaurant*
el servicio de atención al cliente	*customer service*
una sociedad anónima (S.A.)	*limited company (Co. Ltd.)*
una sucursal	*subsidiary*
un supermercado	*supermarket*
un taller	*workshop*
una tienda	*shop*
las ventas al por mayor	*wholesale sales*
las ventas al por menor	*retail sales*

6 El mundo del trabajo *Jobs and work*

¡OTRA VEZ!

● *Activity: Write a list of five jobs. Can you say where they work?*

Por ejemplo:

mecánico - garaje

El mecánico trabaja en un garaje.

6 El mundo del trabajo *Jobs and work*

LA INDUSTRIA Y LAS EMPRESAS DE SERVICIOS
MANUFACTURING AND SERVICE INDUSTRIES

Trabajo en ...	*I work in ...*
Soy aprendiz-a en ...	*I am a trainee in ...*
una fábrica	*a factory*
el sector servicios	*the service industry*
la agricultura	*agriculture*
la banca	*banking*
la Bolsa	*the Stock Market*
el comercio	*commerce*
compras	*buying*
la confección	*clothing*
la construcción de carreteras	*road building*
diseño	*design*
una editorial	*publishing*
electrónica	*the electronics industry*
electrotécnica	*electrical engineering*
energía nuclear	*nuclear power*
la fabricación de herramientas	*tool making*
la horticultura	*horticulture*
hostelería	*catering*
la industria alimenticia	*food*
la industria del automóvil	*the motor industry*
la industria de la construcción	*the construction industry*
la industria del acero	*the steel industry*
la industria del carbón	*the coal industry*
la industria eléctrica	*the power industry*
la industria farmacéutica	*pharmaceutical industry*
la industria médica	*the medical industry*
informática	*computers / information technology*
la ingeniería civil	*civil engineering*
la investigación	*research*
maquinaria	*machinery*
ocio	*leisure*
periodismo	*the press; journalism*
seguros	*insurance*
telecomunicaciones	*telecommunications*
televisión	*television*
transporte	*transport*

transporte marítimo	*shipping*
ventas	*sales*
viajes y turismo	*travel and tourism*

Yo . . .	*I . . .*
ayudo (soy ayudante)	*assist*
coordino	*co-ordinate*
desarrollo	*develop*
diseño	*design*
escribo la correspondencia	*write letters*
fabrico	*manufacture*
hago demostraciones	*demonstrate*
hago el trabajo de oficina	*do the paperwork*
llevo la contabilidad	*do the accounts*
reparto; distribuyo	*distribute*
trabajo en publicidad	*write advertising*
vendo	*sell*

LA INDUSTRIA DE LA CONSTRUCCIÓN
THE CONSTRUCTION INDUSTRY

Los empleos *Jobs*

el albañil	*labourer; bricklayer*
el cantero	*stonemason*
el carpintero	*joiner*
el constructor	*builder*
el electricista	*electrician*
el escayolista	*plasterer*
el fontanero	*plumber*
el pintor decorador	*painter and decorator*
el técnico en calefacciones	*heating engineer*

Los materiales de construcción y las herramientas *Building materials and tools*

el aislamiento	*insulation*
el andamio	*scaffolding*
los azulejos	*wall tiles*
las baldosas	*floor tiles*
el cemento	*cement*
los cimientos	*foundations*
la construcción	*construction*
el cristal	*glass*
la cuerda	*string*
el doble acristalamiento	*double glazing*
la escalera	*ladder*
la escayola	*plaster*
la fibra de vidrio	*glass fibre*
la grava	*gravel*
la hormigonera	*cement mixer*
el ladrillo	*brick*
la madera	*wood*
la madera (de construcción)	*timber*
la medida	*measure*
la piedra	*stone*
la pizarra	*slates*
las tejas	*roof tiles*

La fontanería *Plumbing*

la calefacción	*heating*
las cañerías	*pipes*
el desagüe	*drain*
la ducha	*shower*
el grifo	*tap*
la llave de paso	*stopcock*
los radiadores	*radiators*
el revestimiento	*lagging*
el termo	*boiler*
el termostato	*thermostat*

La electricidad *Electrics*

los accesorios eléctricos	*light fittings*
los amperios	*amps*
la bombilla	*light bulb*
los cables	*wires*
el enchufe	*plug*
el fusible	*fuse*
el interruptor	*switch*
los voltios	*volts*

La pintura y la decoración *Painting and decorating*

el aguarrás	*turps*
el barniz	*varnish*
la brocha	*paint brush*
la escalera	*ladder*
la masilla	*filler*
el papel pintado	*wallpaper*
la pasta adhesiva	*paste*
la pintura	*paint*
la pintura esmalte	*gloss paint*
la pintura mate	*matt paint*
la pintura plástica	*plastic paint*

la pintura preparatoria	*undercoat*
la pulidora; la lijadora	*sander*
la quitapintura	*paint stripper*
el rodillo	*roller*
clavar	*to nail*
construir	*to build*
enyesar; enlucir	*to plaster*
excavar	*to excavate*
lijar	*to sand*
empapelar	*to paper*
martillar; golpear con martillo	*to hammer*
pintar	*to paint*
poner los cimientos	*to lay the foundations*
quitar; desprender	*to strip (wallpaper / paint)*
reparar	*to mend*

Las herramientas *Tools*

la caja de herramientas	*tool box*
el juego de herramientas	*tool kit*
la alargadera	*extension cable*
los alicates	*pliers*
el banco de trabajo	*workbench*
el cable	*cable*
el cepillo de carpintero	*plane*
el cincel	*chisel*
el clavo	*nail*
el destornillador	*screw driver*
el hacha	*axe*
la lijadora	*sander*

la llave (de tuercas)	*spanner*	el tornillo	*screw*
la llave inglesa	*monkey wrench*	la tuerca	*nut*
el martillo	*hammer*		
el mazo	*mallet*	atornillar	*to screw*
el perno	*bolt*	clavar	*to hammer*
el pico	*pick*	destornillar	*to unscrew*
el taladro	*drill*	deshacer;	
el taladro eléctrico	*electric drill*	aflojar	*to undo; loosen*
		taladrar	*to drill*

LA SEGURIDAD EN EL TRABAJO
SAFETY AT WORK

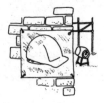

Es obligatorio el uso del casco.
Helmets must be worn at all times.

el accidente	*accident*
el accidente laboral	*industrial accident*
la ambulancia	*ambulance*
la boca de incendios	*fire hydrant*
el bombero	*fireman*
la caída	*fall*
el coche de bomberos	*fire engine*
el cuerpo de bomberos	*fire brigade*
la descarga eléctrica	*electric shock*

Se prohibe (el uso de/el paso ...)	*Do not (use / enter ...)*
¡Peligro!	*Danger!*
¡Atención!	*Warning!*
¡No entrar!	*No entry!*
Prohibido fumar	*Smoking forbidden*
Se prohibe la entrada a toda persona ajena a la obra	*No admittance to unauthorised persons*
Salida	*Exit*
Salida de emergencia	*Emergency exit*
Salida de incendios	*Fire exit*
Punto de Reunión	*Assembly point*
Asistencia médica	*Medical assistance*
Botiquín	*Medical kit*

Rompa el cristal	*Break the glass*
Alarma	*Alarm*
Lávese las manos	*Wash your hands*
Usar...	*Wear...*
guantes	*gloves*
gafas	*goggles*
máscara	*a mask*
ropa	*sterilised*
esterilizada	*clothing*
ropa protectora	*protective clothing*

el extintor	*fire extinguisher*	caerse	*to fall*
el incendio	*fire*	cortarse	*to cut oneself*
los primeros		electrocutarse	*to be electrocuted*
auxilios	*first aid*	necesitar	*to need emergency*
la reanimación	*artificial*	tratamiento	*treatment*
artificial	*resuscitation*	de urgencia	
el seguro	*insurance*	sufrir un	
urgencias	*emergency services*	accidente	*to have an accident*

7 La empresa *The company*

la agencia	agency		el centro médico	medical centre
la empresa;			el depósito	store
la firma	firm		el establecimiento;	
la empresa			el local	premises
privada	private business		los obreros	shop floor
la fábrica	factory		las oficinas	offices
la franquicia	franchise		las oficinas de	
el servicio			plan abierto	open-plan
público	public utility		la recepción	reception
la sociedad			la sala de juntas	boardroom
anónima	limited company		el taller	workshop

EL PERSONAL
THE WORKFORCE

la filial	subsidiary			
la oficina				
central	head office			
la sucursal	branch			

En la oficina *In the office*

las actividades de la			el/la asesor-a	advisor
compañía	operations		el/la ayudante	assistant
el activo;			el/la ayudante	
el haber	assets		personal	personal assistant
el coche de			el/la consultor-a	consultant
la empresa	company car		el/la director-a	
la conferencia;			comercial	commercial
el congreso	conference			manager
el desarrollo	development		el/la director-a de	
las directrices;			la compañía	company director
la política	company policy		el/la director-a	
las ganancias/			financiero-a	financial director
las pérdidas	profit / loss		el/la director-a	
el informe	company report		gerente	managing director
el margen de			el/la interventor-a	
beneficios	profit margin			credit controller
la reunión	company meeting		la junta directiva	board of directors
la transacción	deal		el/la secretario-a	company secretary
			el/la subdirector-a	deputy manager
comprar la			el/la vice-	
parte de	to buy-out		presidente-a	deputy chairman
			el/la agente	
el almacén	warehouse		de seguros	insurance agent
el aparcamiento	car park		el/la archivero-a	filing clerk
los aseos	washrooms		el/la auditor-a	auditor
la cantina	canteen		el/la director-a	manager

la gerencia intermedia	*middle management*		el/la viajante	*commercial traveller*
el guarda jurado	*security guard*		jubilado-a	*retired*
el/la jefe-a	*boss*		la pensión	*pension*
el/la limpiador-a	*cleaner*		el/la pensionista	*pensioner*

el/la mecanó-
grafo-a — *typist*

el/la mecanógrafo-a
de dictáfono — *audio-typist*

el/la taquígrafo-a
— *short-hand typist*

el/la mensajero-a — *courier*

el/la operador-a
de centralita — *switchboard operator*

el/la recepcionista
— *receptionist*

el/la
representante — *representative*

el/la secretario-a — *secretary*

el/la
supervisor-a — *office supervisor*

Los obreros *The shop floor*

el/la aprendiz-a	*apprentice; trainee*
el capataz	*overseer; foreman*
el conserje	*caretaker*
el/la empleado-a	*employee*
el/la empleado-a a tiempo parcial	*part-time employee*
el empresario	*employer*
el/la obrero-a	*worker*
el peón	*labourer*
el/la responsable; jefe de grupo	*team leader*
el técnico	*technician*

Trabajo . . .	*I work . . .*
en turnos	*shifts*
a tiempo completo	*full time*
a tiempo parcial	*part-time*
con horario flexible	*flexitime*
Trabajo en el departamento de . . .	*I work in the . . . department*
administración	*administration*
compras	*buying / procurement*
contabilidad	*accounts*
control de calidad	*quality control*
exportación	*export*
fabricación	*manufacturing*
importación	*import*
mecanografía	*typing pool*
personal	*personnel*
publicidad	*publicity*
ventas/márketing	*sales / marketing*

7 La empresa *The company*

Ventas *Sales*

el análisis	*analysis*
el comerciante exclusivo	*sole agency, exclusivity*
el/la competidor-a	*competidor*
la compra	*purchase*
la concesión	*concession*
las condiciones de pago	*payment terms*
el/la consumidor-a	*consumer*
los contactos	*contacts*
el descuento	*discount*
el/la detallista; el/la comerciante al por menor	*retailer*
la distribución	*distribution*
la documentación	*documentation*
las exportaciones	*exports*
la garantía	*guarantee*
las importaciones	*imports*
libre de gastos de envío	*franco (delivered 'free'with all duties paid)*
el/la mayorista	*wholesaler*
el mercado nacional	*home market*
la muestra	*sample*
el negocio; el comercio	*business*
la oferta	*offer*
el ordenador	*computer*
la pieza	*component*
el pedido	*order*
el porcentaje	*percentage*
el presupuesto	*quotation*
la reclamación	*complaint*
el rendimiento	*performance*
la representación; la concesión	*dealership*
el tanto por ciento	*percent*
las ventas por correo	*mail order*
el viaje de negocios	*business journey*

Contabilidad *Accounts*

a crédito	*in credit*
el/la acreedor-a	*creditor*
el banco de compensación	*clearing bank*
la carta de crédito	*letter of credit*
el certificado de seguro	*insurance certificate*
el código bancario	*bank code*
el comprobante	*voucher*
las condiciones de crédito	*credit terms*
las condiciones de pago	*payment terms*
el coste	*cost*
el coste, seguro y flete	*CIF (carriage, insurance and freight)*
los costes fijos	*fixed costs*
el crédito	*credit*
la cuenta	*account*
el depósito	*deposit*
el/la deudor-a	*debtor*
el estado de cuenta	*statement*
el expediente	*file*
la expiración	*expiry*

7 La empresa *The company*

las facilidades crediticias	*credit facilities*	la demora	*delay*
la factura	*bill; invoice*	disponible	*available*
la fecha límite	*deadline*	no disponible	*not available*
las finanzas	*finance*	el documento	*document*
franco fábrica	*ex-works*	en depósito	*in storage*
franco; gratis; libre de gastos	*free*	en existencias	*in stock*
el gasto; el desembolso	*expenditure*	fuera de existencias	*out of stock*
los honorarios	*fee*	el envío	*despatch*
la indemnización	*compensation*	la entrega en fecha futura	*forward delivery*
la liquidación	*settlement*	el equipamiento	*equipment*
en metálico; en efectivo	*cash*	el excedente	*excess*
la nota de entrega	*delivery note*	los gastos de transporte	*transport costs*
el número de referencia	*reference number*	la letra de cambio	*bill of exchange*
el organigrama	*flow chart*	la licencia	*permit*
el pago	*payment*	las mercancías	*freight* (goods)
la pérdida	*loss*	la red	*network*
la quiebra; la bancarrota	*bankruptcy*	pasado-a de fecha	*out of date*
el recibo	*receipt*	el peso	*weight*
el reembolso; la devolución	*refund*	la remesa	*consignment*
la referencia	*reference*	el tamaño	*size*
el saldo	*balance*	el transbordo	*transshipment*
		el tránsito; el paso	*transit*
		el transporte	*shipment*
		el transporte	*transport*
		válido-a	*valid*

Envíos *Despatch*

las aduanas	*customs*
el/la agente expedidor	*freight forwarder*
el almacén	*depot*
los bienes; las mercancías	*goods*
la carga	*freight* (load)
el conocimiento de embarque	*bill of lading*
el contenedor	*container*

EL MÁRKETING Y LA PRODUCCIÓN
MARKETING AND PRODUCTION

el análisis	*research*
el análisis de mercados	*market research*
el arancel	*tariff*

las barreras arancelarias	*trade barriers*	las materias primas	*raw materials*
la calidad	*quality*	las negociaciones	*negotiations; talks*
la cámara de comercio	*chamber of commerce*	el/la negociador-a	*negotiator*
la campaña de ventas	*sales campaign*	el objetivo	*target*
la cantidad	*quantity*	la opción	*option*
el comercio	*trade; commerce*	el pago	*payment*
la compra	*purchase*	la planta; la fábrica	*plant*
las condiciones	*terms*	el presupuesto	*estimate; budget*
el contrato	*contract*	la producción	*output*
el control de calidad	*quality control*	el producto nacional bruto	*gross national product*
la cuota	*quota*	el programa	*schedule*
los derechos de entrada	*import duty*	el progreso; la evolución	*progress*
el director comercial	*marketing manager*	la promoción	*promotion*
la distribución	*distribution*	la promoción de ventas	*sales promotion*
el equipo; la maquinaria	*machinery*	el pronóstico de mercados	*market forecast*
el equipo de ventas	*sales team*	el proyecto	*project*
el excedente	*surplus*	la publicidad	*publicity*
la fabricación en serie	*mass production*	el punto de venta	*point of sale*
el/la fabricante	*manufacturer*	la regulación	*regulation*
la gama de productos	*range of goods*	la renovación	*renewal*
la gestión	*management*	la responsabilidad	*liability*
el informe	*report*	las restricciones arancelarias	*trade restrictions*
el/la intérprete	*interpreter*	las tendencias de mercado	*market trends*
la licencia	*licence*	la transferencia	*transfer*
el líder del mercado	*market leader*		
el logotipo	*logo*	(a) largo plazo	*long term*
la marca registrada	*trademark*	(a) corto plazo	*short term*
el márketing	*marketing*	hecho-a a mano	*handmade*
		oficial; autorizado-a	*official*

producido-a en serie	mass produced
el cartel	poster
el catálogo	catalogue
la exposición	exhibition
el/la expositor-a	exhibitor
la feria de muestras	trade fair
el folleto	brochure
la promoción	promotion
el stand	stand
administrar	to manage
comprar	to buy
dejar sin trabajo	to make redundant
despedir	to sack
dirigir	to direct
enviar	to send
exportar	to export
importar	to import
jubilarse	to retire
nombrar	to appoint
pagar	to pay
promover	to promote
repartir; entregar	to deliver
seleccionar; elegir	to select
transportar	to transport
vender	to sell

EN LA OFICINA
IN THE OFFICE

Material de oficina y mobiliario
Equipment

el archivador	filing cabinet
el bolígrafo	pen; biro
el borrador; la goma	rubber; eraser

el cajón	drawer
la calculadora	calculator
el calendario	calendar
la chincheta	drawing pin
la cinta adhesiva	sticky tape
el clip	paper clip
el diccionario	dictionary
el dictáfono	dictating machine
la entrada/salida de documentos	in- / out-tray
el escritorio	desk
las etiquetas adhesivas	sticky labels
el expediente	file
el fax	fax machine
la fotocopiadora	photocopier
la franqueadora	franking machine
la grapadora	stapler
las grapas	staples
la impresora	printer
el lápiz	pencil
la máquina de café	coffee machine
la máquina de escribir	typewriter
la mesa	table
el ordenador	computer
el papel	paper
el papel cello	sellotape
la papelera	waste bin
el pegamento	glue
la regla	ruler
los sellos	stamps
la silla giratoria	swivel chair
el sobre	envelope
la taladradora	hole punch
el teléfono	telephone
las tijeras	scissors
la trituradora	shredder
el ventilador	ventilator

7 La empresa *The company*

El ordenador *The computer*

la base de datos	*database*	la memoria	*memory*
el camino	*path*	la memoria RAM	*RAM*
el CD ROM	*CD-ROM*	la memoria ROM	*ROM*
la cinta	*tape*	el menú	*menu*
el correo electrónico	*electronic mail*	el módem	*modem*
el cursor	*cursor*	el monitor	*monitor*
el disco duro	*hard disk*	el multimedia	*multimedia*
el disquete	*disquette*	la pantalla	*screen*
el escáner	*scanner*	el procesador de textos	*word processor*
la hoja de cálculo	*spreadsheet*	el procesamiento de textos	*word processing*
el icono	*icon*	el programa	*programme*
la impresora	*printer*	el ratón	*mouse*
la instalación	*installation*	la tecla	*key*
el interruptor	*switch*	el teclado	*keyboard*
el lector	*drive*	la terminal	*terminal*
el lector CD-ROM	*CD-ROM drive*	la ventana	*window*
		el virador	*toner*
		el virus	*virus*

No funciona. ¿Cómo se ... ?	*It doesn't work. How do you ... ?*
apaga	*switch off*
enciende	*switch on*
entra	*enter*
entra en el programa	*get into the programme*
guarda	*save*
hace back up	*back-up*
hace clic	*click*
pulsa	*press*
instala	*instal*
subraya	*underline*
teclea	*key in*
vuelve a rellenar	*re-fill*

¡OTRA VEZ!

● *Activity:* Diga los nombres de los objetos en esta oficina. *Label the objects in this office.*

EL TELÉFONO
THE TELEPHONE

la centralita	*switchboard*
el contestador	*answering*
automático	*machine*
la extensión	*extension*
la guía	
telefónica	*telephone directory*
el localizador personal;	
el busca	*pager*
el módem	*modem*
el teléfono	*phone*
el teléfono móvil	*mobile phone*
el teléfono	
analógico	*analogue phone*
el teléfono	
digital	*digital phone*
el teléfono móvil	
del coche	*car phone*
el fax	*fax*
la información	*directory enquiries*
la llamada a cobro	
revertido	*reverse charge call*
el mensaje;	
el recado	*message*
el número de	
teléfono	*phone number*
el prefijo	*dialling code*
el tono de	
marcar	*dialling tone*
(estar)	
comunicando	*engaged*
no funciona	*out of order*

7 La empresa *The company*

AL TELÉFONO *ON THE PHONE*

¡Diga!	*Hello!*
¿En qué puedo ayudarle?	*Can I help you?*
¿Puedo hablar con ...?	*Can I speak to ...?*
¿Puede ponerme con la extensión ...?	*Can I have extension ...?*
¡Un momento!	*Hold on!*
El/ella no está	*He / she is not there.*
El/ella está hablando.	*He / she is on the other line.*
¿Puede llamarme luego?	*Can he / she / you call back later?*
¿Puedo coger/dejar un mensaje?	*Can I take / leave a message?*
Gracias por su llamada.	*Thank you for calling.*
De nada.	*Don't mention it.*
Lo siento, me he confundido de número.	*I'm sorry, I've got the wrong number.*
¿Cómo se escribe?	*Can you spell it?*
¿Puede repetir?	*Can you repeat it?*
¿Puede hablar más despacio?	*Can you speak more slowly?*
Deje su mensaje después de la señal.	*Leave a message after the tone.*
Llame después de ...	*Ring after ...*
Es urgente.	*It's urgent.*

llamar	*to call*	telefonear	*to phone*
mandar un fax	*to send a fax*	volver a llamar	*to call back*

CITAS Y EXCUSAS
ARRANGING MEETINGS AND MAKING EXCUSES

¿Dónde nos vemos?	*Where shall we meet?*
Nos vemos ...	*Let's meet ...*
en el aparcamiento	*in the car park*
en el bar	*in the bar*
en el campo de golf	*on the golf course*
en mi casa	*at my house*
en el cruce de ...	*at the junction of ...*
en frente de la estación	*opposite the station*
en la estación	*at the station*
en el hotel	*in the hotel*

7 **La empresa** *The company*

en mi/tu oficina	*in my/your office*
en recepción	*at reception*
en el restaurante	*at the restaurant*
en el vestíbulo	*in the foyer*

Yo te recogeré.	*I'll pick you up.*
¿Cuándo nos vemos?	*When shall we meet?*
a las diez	*at 10 o'clock*
dentro de media hora	*in half an hour*
dentro de cinco minutos	*in five minutes*
mañana	*tomorrow*
Lo siento.	*I'm sorry.*
No quiero.	*I don't want to.*
No puedo.	*I can't.*

No tengo tiempo.	*I haven't the time.*
Tengo demasiado trabajo.	*I have too much work.*
No me interesa.	*I'm not interested.*
Tengo una cita/un compromiso.	*I have an appointment.*
Estoy ocupado-a	*I'm busy.*
Tengo que ir . . .	*I have to go to . . .*
al dentista	*the dentist*
al médico	*the doctor*
al hospital	*the hospital*

¡OTRA VEZ!

● *Activity:* Lo siento, no puedo . . . *I'm sorry, I can't make it, I . . .*

8 El arte y los medios de comunicación *Art and the media*

EL ARTE Y LOS ARTISTAS
ART AND ARTISTS

El arte *Art*

el/la artista	*artist*
la colección	*art collection*
el/la diseñador-a	*designer*
la exposición	*art exhibition*
el/la grafista	*graphic artist*
el/la ilustrador-a	*illustrator*
el museo de bellas artes	*art gallery*

El dibujo y la pintura
Drawing and painting

la acuarela	*water colour*
el apunte	*sketch*
el bodegón	*still life*
el caballete	*easel*
el carboncillo	*charcoal*
el cuadro	*picture*
el dibujo	*drawing*
el lápiz	*crayon*
el lienzo	*canvas*
el marco	*picture frame*
el óleo	*oil painting*
el paisaje	*landscape*
el pastel	*pastels*
el pincel	*paint brush*
la pintura	*painting*
las pinturas	*paints*
el retrato	*portrait*

La cerámica y la escultura
Pottery and sculpture

el/la alfarero-a; el/la ceramista	*potter*
la alfarería; la cerámica	*pottery*

el barniz	*varnish*
el barro	*clay*
la maceta/ el tiesto	*pot*
el torno	*wheel*

el/la escultor-a	*sculptor*
la escultura	*sculpture*
el busto	*bust*
el cincel	*chisel*
el estudio; el taller	*studio*
el/la modelo	*model*
la talla	*carving*
el vaciado	*cast*

la artesanía	*craftmanship*
el/la artesano-a	*craftsman*

La arquitectura *Architecture*

el/la arquitecto	*architect*
el edificio	*building*
los planos	*plans*

barroco	*Baroque*
clásico	*Classic*
gótico	*Gothic*
mudéjar	*Mudejar* (Arab style under Catholic rule)
plateresco	*Plateresque*
románico	*Roman*

cocer	*to fire*
colorear	*to colour*
dibujar	*to draw*
diseñar	*to design*
esculpir	*to sculpt*
exponer	*to exhibit*
hacer un boceto	*to sketch*
pintar	*to paint*
tallar	*to carve*
tornear	*to throw*

LA PALABRA ESCRITA: LOS LIBROS, LAS REVISTAS, LOS PERIÓDICOS
THE WRITTEN WORD: BOOKS, MAGAZINES, NEWSPAPERS

el/la articulista; cronista	*feature writer*
el/la autor-a	*author*
el/la biógrafo-a	*biographer*
la casa editorial	*publisher*
el/la diseñador-a	*designer*
el/la diseñador-a gráfico	*graphic designer*
el/la fotógrafo-a	*photographer*
el/la historiador-a	*historian*
el/la novelista	*novelist*
el/la periodista	*journalist*
el/la poeta	*poet*
los derechos de autor	*royalties; copyright*
la escritura	*hand writing*
la máquina de escribir	*typewriter*
el procesador de textos	*word processor*
el cómic	*comic*
el libro	*book*
el periódico; el diario	*newspaper*
la revista	*magazine*
diario	*daily*
semanal	*weekly*
quincenal	*bi-weekly*
mensual	*monthly*
la autobiografía	*autobiography*
la biografía	*biography*
la ciencia ficción	*science fiction*
el diccionario	*dictionary*
el documento	*document*
la enciclopedia	*encyclopaedia*
el folleto	*brochure*
el libro/la edición de bolsillo	*pocket book*
el libro de frases	*phrase book*
el libro de referencia	*reference book*
el libro de texto	*text book*
el libro de viajes	*travel book*
la novela de suspense; de misterio	*thriller*
la novela negra	*crime story*
el relato; el cuento	*short story*
el relato de detectives	*detective story*
el artículo	*article*
el bolígrafo	*pen*
el capítulo	*chapter*
la carta	*letter (correspondence)*
el cuento; la historia	*story*
el cuento de hadas	*fairy tale*
el ejemplar	*volume*
el/la escritor-a	*writer*
la ficción	*fiction*
la frase; la oración	*sentence*
la frase; la expresión	*phrase*
la guía	*guide book*
el horóscopo	*horoscope*
la idea general	*outline*
el índice	*index*
el índice de materias	*contents*

la lámina; la ilustración	*illustration*
la letra	*letter* (of alphabet)
la leyenda	*legend*
la línea	*line*
el manual	*manual*
el libro de consulta	*handbook*
la novela	*novel*
la novela histórica	*historical novel*
la obra de teatro	*play*
la página	*page*
la palabra	*word*
el papel	*paper*
el párrafo	*paragraph*
la pluma	*fountain pen*
el poema	*poem*
la poesía	*poetry*
la portada	*cover*
la cubierta	*hard cover*
el libro de bolsillo	*paper back*
el prospecto	*leaflet*
el serial; la novela por entregas	*serial*
la tinta	*ink*

La prensa *Newspapers*

los anuncios	*advertisements*
los anuncios por palabras	*small ads.*
el artículo	*article*
la Bolsa	*stock market report*
las cartas al director	*letters to the editor*
la cartelera	*what's on*
la composición	*layout*
el consultorio	*problem page*
el crucigrama	*crossword*
la cultura	*arts*

los deportes	*sport*
la economía	*financial news*
el editorial; el artículo de fondo	*editorial*
las farmacias de guardia	*emergency chemists*
el humor	*cartoons*
el jeroglífico	*puzzles*
las necrológicas	*obituaries*
la política	*politics*
la primera plana	*front page*
la revista	*reviews*
sociedad	*social*
el suplemento	*supplement*
los teléfonos de urgencia	*emergency telephone numbers*
la televisión/ radio	*television / radio*
el tiempo	*weather report*
los titulares	*headlines*
los toros; la lidia	*bullfight reports*
regional	*local news*
nacional	*national news*
internacional	*international news*

La opinión *Opinion*

el cuestionario	*questionnaire*
la desventaja	*disadvantage*
la diferencia	*difference*
la encuesta	*survey*
la semejanza	*similarity*
la ventaja	*advantage*
brevemente	*in short*
creer	*to believe*
depende de	*it depends*
de todas formas	*all the same*
extraordinario-a	*extraordinary*
habitual; corriente	*usual*
para terminar	*in conclusion*

pensar	*to think*
poco habitual;	
poco corriente	*unusual*
por otra parte	*on the other hand*
por último	*finally*
por una parte	*on the one hand*
se trata de	*it's a question of;*
	it's about
sin comentarios	*no comment*
según los sondeos	
de opinión	*according to the polls*

dudar	*to doubt*
estar	
equivocado	*to be wrong*
preferir	*to prefer*
ser necesario	*to be necessary*
tener razón	*to be right*

el acento	*accent (´)*
la diéresis	*diaeresis (¨)*
la tilde	*tilde (~)*

la coma	*comma*
las comillas	*inverted commas*
los dos puntos	*colon*
el guión	*hyphen*
el paréntesis	*brackets*
el punto	*full stop*
el punto y coma	*semi-colon*
el signo de	
admiración	*exclamation mark*
el signo de	
interrogación	*question mark*
el tipo de letra	*font*

cursiva	*italic*
negrita	*bold*

corregir	*to correct*
corregir las	
pruebas	*to proof read*
escribir	*to write*
escribir a	
máquina	*to type*
imprimir	*to print*
leer	*to read*
preparar para	
la imprenta	*to edit*
publicar por	
entregas	*to serialise*
puntuar	*to punctuate*
sangrar	*to indent*
usar	
mayúsculas	*to use capital letters*
usar minúsculas	*to use small letters*

EL CINE Y EL TEATRO
CINEMA AND THEATRE

El cine *The cinema*

la banda sonora	*sound track*
el cine	*cinema*
la entrada	*ticket*
la fila	*row*
la localidad;	
la butaca	*seat*
la pantalla	*screen*
el pase	*performance*
el pasillo	*aisle*
la película;	
el filme	*film*
el público	*audience*
la taquilla	*ticket office*
el vestíbulo	*foyer*

Los géneros de las películas *Film types*

la película ...	... *(film)*
de amor	*love story*
de ciencia ficción	*science fiction*
de detectives	*detective*
de guerra	*war*
de miedo	*horror film*
de suspense	*thriller*
del espacio	*space*
del oeste	*western*
pornográfica	*pornographic*
romántica	*romance*
violenta	*violent*

censurada	*censored*	el actor/la actriz	*actor / actress*
cortada	*cut*	el/la ayudante de	
doblada	*dubbed*	producción	*assistant producer*
muda	*silent*	el cámara	*cameraman*
subtitulada	*sub-titled*	el/la director-a	*director*
		el/la estrella	
una comedia	*comedy*	de cine	*film star*
en versión	*original version*	el/la productor-a	*producer*
original	(subtitled)	el/la técnico de	
		sonido	*sound technician*
no aconsejada	*Not suitable for*	trataba de ...	*It was about ...*
para menores	*people under*		
de ...	*... years*		

Era una película ...	*It was a ... film*
buena	*good*
emocionante	*exciting*
mala	*bad*
horrible	*awful*
aburrida	*boring*
Estaba bien/mal rodada.	*It was well / badly filmed.*
(No) la recomendaría.	*I would (not) recommend it.*
Quisiera dos entradas para ...	*I would like two tickets for...*
No hay entradas; localidades	*It's sold out.*
Quisiera reservar ...	*I would like to book ...*

El teatro *The theatre*

el anfiteatro	*circle*
el auditorio	*auditorium*
los bastidores	*wings*
las butacas	*stalls*
las candilejas	*footlights*
el decorado	*scenery*
el escenario	*stage*
el guardarropa	*cloakroom*
las luces	*lights*
el paraíso	*balcony*
el palco	*box*
la salida	*exit*
la salida de emergencia	*emergency exit*
el telón	*curtain*
la tribuna	*gallery*

La obra — The play

el actor	*actor*
la actriz	*actress*
los aplausos	*applause*
el argumento; la trama	*plot*
el/la crítico-a	*critic*
los decorados	*set*
el entreacto; el intermedio	*interval*
la escena	*scene*
la función	*show*
la función de tarde	*matinee*
el maquillaje	*make-up*
el miedo al público	*stage fright*
el nerviosismo	*nerves*
la noche del estreno	*first-night*
el papel	*part; role*
el personaje	*character*
el primer acto	*act 1*

la producción	*production*
el programa	*programme*
la reseña	*review*
el traje	*costume*

La ópera *Opera*

el coro	*chorus*
el/la director-a (de orquesta)	*conductor*
la orquesta	*orchestra*
el reparto	*cast*
el/la solista	*soloist*

El ballet *Ballet*

el/la bailarín-a	*ballet dancer*
el coreógrafo	*choreographer*
el cuerpo de ballet	*corps de ballet*
la prima ballerina	*prima ballerina*

El drama *Drama*

el/la apuntador-a	*prompt (-er)*
el/la director-a de escena	*stage manager*
el escenógrafo	*designer*
el/la primera figura	*star*
el/la productor-a	*producer*
el/la suplente	*understudy*

El circo *Circus*

el/la acróbata	*acrobat*
los animales amaestrados	*performing animals*
el/la artista	*artist*
la carpa	*big top*

el payaso	*clown*
la pista	*ring*
el/la trapecista	*trapeze artist*
la comedia	*comedy*
el drama	
histórico	*historical drama*
la farsa	*farce*
el musical	*musical*
la revista	*review*
los títeres	*puppet show*
actuar	*to perform*
bailar	*to dance*
hacer el	
papel de	*to play the role of*
representar	*to act*
tomar la	
delantera	*to take the lead*
abuchear	*to boo*
aplaudir	*to clap*
disfrutar/pasarlo	
bien	*to enjoy*
mirar	*to watch*
(no) gustar	*(not) to like*

La música *Music*

el/la cantante	*singer*
el/la intérprete	*player*
los instrumentos	*instruments*
el músico	*musician*

La música pop *Pop music*

el acorde	*chord*
las altavoces	*loudspeakers*
los amplifica-	
dores	*amplifiers*
el bajo	*bass guitar*
el batería	*drummer*

la batería	*drums*
el conjunto	*band*
los 40	
principales	*Top 40*
el disc jockey; el	
pinchadiscos	*disc jockey*
el empresario;	
el agente	*impresario*
la estrella	
de pop	*pop star*
un éxito musical	*hit*
el grupo	*group*
la guitarra	*guitar*
el/la	
guitarrista	*guitarist*
la melodía	*tune*
el teclado	*keyboard*
el rock	*rock*
el pop	*pop*
el country	*country*
and western	*and western*
el folk	*folk*
el jazz	*jazz*
el flamenco	*flamenco*

La música clásica *Classical music*

el/la	
acompañante	*accompanist*
el/la cantante	*singer*
el/la	
compositor-a	*composer*
el coro	*choir*
la orquesta	*orchestra*
la partitura	*score*
el/la pianista	*pianist*
barítono	*bass*
contralto	*alto*
soprano	*soprano*
tiple	*treble*

8 El arte y los medios de comunicación *Art and the media*

Los instrumentos *Instruments*

Los instrumentos de cuerda **Strings**

el arpa	*harp*
el banjo	*banjo*
el contrabajo	*double bass*
la guitarra	*guitar*
la viola	*viola*
el violín	*violin*
el violoncelo	*cello*

Los instrumentos de aire **Wind instruments**

el clarinete	*clarinet*
la flauta	*flute*
el oboe	*oboe*
el saxofón	*saxophone*
el trombón	*trombone*
la trompa	*horn*
la trompeta	*trumpet*
la tuba	*tuba*

Los instrumentos de percusión **Percussion**

las castañuelas	*castanets*
la pandereta	*tamborine*
el tambor	*drum*
el tamboril	*side drum*
el timbal	*kettle drum*
el triángulo	*triangle*
el clavicordio	*harpsichord*
el órgano	*organ*
el piano	*piano*

el/la primer violín	*leader*
el/la solista	*soloist*
el solo	*solo*
el dúo	*duet*
la orquesta de cámara	*chamber orchestra*
el cassette	*cassette recorder*
el CD	*CD*
la cinta	*cassette*
el disco	*record*
el lector de CD	*CD player*
el micrófono	*microphone*
el tocadiscos	*record player*

La escala *The scale*

el tono	*key*
desafinado	*flat*
agudo/sostenido	*sharp*
mayor	*major*
menor	*minor*
afinado	*in tune*
tener oído perfecto	*to have perfect pitch*
un/una buen-a/mal-a músico-a	*a good / poor musician*
una buena/ mala voz	*a good / poor voice*
afinar	*to tune*
cantar	*to sing*
grabar	*to record; tape*
rasguear	*to strum*
tocar	*to play*

8 El arte y los medios de comunicación *Art and the media*

LA RADIO Y LA TELEVISIÓN
RADIO AND TELEVISION

la televisión/TV	*TV*
la radio	*radio*
la antena	*aerial*
la audiencia	*audience*
la cadena	*channel*
el cámara	*cameraman*
la cámara de vídeo	*video camera*
el corresponsal	*correspondant*
el/la editor-a	*editor*
la entrevista	*interview*
la grabación	*recording*
el ingeniero de sonido	*sound engineer*
la interferencia	*interference*
el mando a distancia	*remote control*
las noticias; el informativo	*news broadcast*
el/la oyente	*listener*
el/la presentador-a	*presenter*
el/la productor-a	*producer*
el programa en directo	*live programme*
los rótulos	*credits*
el/la televidente	*viewer*
la televisión por cable	*cable TV*
la televisión por satélite	*satellite TV*

el vídeo	*video recorder*
los anuncios	*commercials*
la comedia	*comedy*
el concurso	*games show*
los dibujos animados	*cartoon*
el documental	*documentary*
el programa	*programme*
el programa de viajes	*travel show*
el reality show	*tabloid TV show*
la retransmisión	*repeat*
la telenovela	*soap*
el programa de entrevistas/ la tertulia	*chat show*
apagar	*to switch off*
averiarse	*to break down*
borrar	*to wipe off*
cambiar de cadena	*to change channels*
encender	*to switch on*
grabar	*to record*
poner	*to play back*
sintonizar	*to tune*
¿Viste . . . ?	*Did you see . . . ?*
¿Has visto . . . ?	*Have you seen . . . ?*
¿Qué te pareció . . . ?	*What did you think of . . . ?*

9 El ocio y los deportes *Hobbies and sports*

EL OCIO
LEISURE

Los lugares de reunión
Venues

el bar	*bar*
el bingo	*bingo hall*
la bolera	*bowling alley*
el casino	*casino*
el circo	*circus*
el club	*club*
el club juvenil	*youth club*
la discoteca	*disco*

el estadio	*stadium*
la feria de atracciones	*fun fair*
la fiesta	*party*
el hipódromo	*race course*
el night club	*night club*
el parque	*park*
el parque temático	*theme park*
la piscina	*swimming pool*
la pista de hielo	*ice rink*
la sala de conciertos	*concert hall*

Me gusta(-n)...	*I like...*
las actividades al aire libre	*outdoor pursuits*
bailar	*dancing*
coleccionar	*collecting*
sellos	*stamps*
postales	*postcards*
reproducciones de...	*model...*
coser	*sewing*
dibujar	*drawing*
escuchar música	*listening to music*
hacer footing	*jogging*
hacer punto	*knitting*
leer	*reading*
montar a caballo	*horse riding*
montar en bicicleta	*cycling*
nadar	*swimming*
pasear	*walking*
pescar	*fishing*
pintar	*painting*
tocar un instrumento musical	*playing music*
el bricolaje	*D.I.Y*
la fotografía	*photography*
la jardinería	*gardening*
el senderismo	*hiking*

9 El ocio y los deportes *Hobbies and sports*

Salir *Going out*

Me gusta ir . . .	*I like going to . . .*
al cine	*the cinema*
a la discoteca	*discos*
a una fiesta	*parties*
a un polideportivo	*the sports centre*
al restaurante	*restaurants*
al teatro	*the theatre*

Me gusta (jugar al tenis).	*I like (playing tennis).*
Me gustaría (jugar al tenis).	*I would like (to play tennis).*
Prefiero (salir a tomar una copa).	*I prefer (to go for a drink).*
No me gusta (jugar al tenis).	*I don't like (playing tennis).*
Odio (jugar al tenis).	*I hate (playing tennis).*

LOS PASATIEMPOS
HOBBIES

Las cartas, el ajedrez y los juegos de mesa
Cards, chess and board games

el ajedrez	*chess*
el juego de cartas	*card game*
el juego de mesa	*board game*

Las cartas *Cards*

la baraja de cartas	*pack of cards*
el palo	*suit*
los corazones	*hearts*
los diamantes	*diamonds*
las picas	*spades*
los tréboles	*clubs*
el as	*ace*
el comodín	*joker*

la reina; la dama	*queen*
el rey	*king*
la sota	*jack*
el triunfo	*trump*
el bridge	*bridge*
la canasta	*canasta*
el póker	*poker*
el whist	*whist*
el mus	*popular Spanish card game*
el/la jugador-a	*player*
jugar	*to play*
Te toca a ti.	*It's your turn.*

El ajedrez *Chess*

el alfil	*bishop*
el caballo	*knight*
el peón	*pawn*
la reina	*queen*
el rey	*king*
la torre	*castle / rook*

blanco	*white*
negro	*black*
jaque	*check*
jaque mate	*checkmate*
mover	*to move*
Te toca mover a ti.	*It's your move.*
enrocar	*to castle*
¡jaque!	*check!*
¡jaque mate!	*check mate!*
¡No puedes hacer eso!	*You can't do that!*
Tienes que . . .	*You have to . . .*

Otros juegos *Other games*

los dados	*dice*
las damas	*draughts*
el dominó	*dominoes*
la oca	*Spanish 'snakes and ladders'*
el parchís	*parcheesi*
la casilla	*'square'*
la pieza	*'man'*
el reloj automático	*timer*
el tablero	*board*
la lotería	*lottery*
el cupón (de los ciegos)	*lottery ticket (for ONCE-association for the blind)*
el décimo	*lottery ticket*
el gordo	*jackpot*
el número del décimo	*lottery number*
el número premiado	*winning number*
el premio	*lottery prize*
la quiniela	*football pools*
el sorteo	*draw*

BAILAR *DANCING*

el baile disco	*disco*
el baile folklórico	*folk / country dancing*
el baile swing	*jive*
el merengue	*merengue*
la salsa	*salsa*
el tango	*tango*
el vals	*waltz*
la sala de baile	*ballroom*

Bailes folklóricos españoles *Spanish folk dances*

el flamenco	(Andalucía)
la jota	(Aragón/La Mancha)
la muñeira	(Galicia)
las sevillanas	(Andalucía)
la sardana	(Cataluña)
el compás	*beat*
la pareja	*partner*
el paso	*step*
el ritmo	*rhythm*

LA PESCA *FISHING*

el agua salada	*salt water*
el agua dulce	*fresh water*
la pesca (con caña)	*angling*
la pesca (con mosca)	*fly fishing*
la pesca de agua dulce	*coarse fishing*
el pez – los peces	*fish*
el anzuelo	*hook*
la barca	*boat*
las botas altas de goma	*waders*

la caña	*rod*
el cebo	*bait*
la cesta	*basket*
la cuchara	*landing net*
la mosca seca	*dry fly*
la mosca	*fly*
el peso	*weight*
la red	*net*
los remos	*oars*
el sedal	*line*
la silla de tijera	*stool*

Los peces de agua dulce
Freshwater fish

la perca	*perch*
el salmón	*salmon*
la trucha	*trout*

Los peces de mar *Sea fish*

el arenque	*herring*
el atún	*tuna*
el bacalao	*cod*
la caballa	*mackerel*
los calamares	*squid*
el cazón	*dogfish*
el choco	*cuttlefish*
la merluza	*hake*
la pescadilla	*whiting*
el pez espada	*swordfish*
el pulpo	*octopus*
el rape	*angler fish*
la sardina	*sardine*
el tiburón	*shark*

Los mariscos *Shellfish*

las almejas	*clams*
los berberechos	*cockles*
el camarón	*shrimp*
el cangrejo	*crab*

la cigala	*Dublin bay prawn (scampi)*
la gamba	*prawn*
la langosta	*lobster*
el langostino	*large prawn*
los mejillones	*mussels*
las vieiras	*scallops*
pescar	*to fish*
capturar	*to catch*

LA EQUITACIÓN
HORSES AND RIDING

el caballo	*horse*
el poney	*pony*
el semental	*stallion*
la yegua	*mare*
los arneses	*harness*
la brida	*bridle*
la cuadra	*stable*
el estribo	*stirrup*
la explanada de ensillado; el paddock	*paddock*
el salto	*jump*
la silla de montar	*saddle*
las botas de montar	*riding boots*
la chaqueta de montar	*riding coat*
la fusta	*crop*
la gorra de montar	*riding hat*
los pantalones de montar	*jodhpurs*
apostar	*to bet*
la apuesta	*bet*
las carreras de caballos	*horse racing*

la carrera de caballos	
sin obstáculos	*flat race*
el corredor	
de apuestas	*bookie*
el/la ganador-a	*winner*
el hipódromo	*race course*
el jockey	*jockey*
caerse	*to fall off*
cuidar los	
caballos	*to groom*
ganar	*to win*
ir al trote	*to trot*
montar a caballo	*to ride*

LA FOTOGRAFÍA
PHOTOGRAPHY

la abertura	*aperture*
el álbum	*album*
la ampliación	*enlargement*
automático-a	*automatic*
en blanco	
y negro	*black and white*
la bombilla	
de flash	*flash bulb*
en color	*colour*

la composición	*setting*
la copia	*copy; print*
el cuarto oscuro	*dark room*
la diapositiva	*slide*
la exposición	
insuficiente	*under exposure*
el exposímetro	*exposure meter*
el flash	*flash*
el/la fotógrafo	*photographer*
el fotómetro	*light meter*
granangular	*wide angle*
la máquina	
(fotográfica)	*camera*
mate/brillo	*matt / glossy*
el negativo	*negative*
el objetivo	*lens*
la película	
rápida/lenta	*fast / slow film*
la pila	*battery*
la tapa del	
objetivo	*lens cap*
el teleobjetivo	*telephoto lens*
el tiempo de	*exposure time*
revelado	*(developing)*
el trípode	*tripod*
el visor	*view finder*

El rebobinador/el flash no funciona.	*The winder / flash doesn't work.*

ampliar	*to enlarge*
enfocar	*to focus*
exponer	*to expose*
hacer copias	*to print*

rebobinar	*to re-wind*
revelar	*to develop*
sacar una foto	*to take a photo*

9 El ocio y los deportes *Hobbies and sports*

LOS DEPORTES – GENERAL
SPORTS – GENERAL

el auto- movilismo	*motor racing*
el balonmano	*handball*
el billar	*billiards; pool*
el juego de bolos	*skittles*
la lucha libre	*wrestling*
el monopatín	*skate boarding*
el motociclismo	*motorcycle racing*
el patinaje sobre ruedas	*roller skating*
el rugby	*rugby*
el squash	*squash*
el voleibol	*volleyball*

Las artes marciales
Martial arts

el judo	*judo*
el tae kwando	*tae kwando*
el cinturón	*belt*
el traje	*suit*

El bádminton *Badminton*

la raqueta	*racquet*
la red	*net*
el volante	*shuttlecock*
la pista	*court*

El baloncesto *Basketball*

el cesto	*basket*

Los bolos *Bowls*

el boliche	*jack*

El boxeo *Boxing*

el asalto	*round*

los guantes de boxeo	*gloves*
el K.O.	*knockout*
el ring	*ring*

Los dardos *Darts*

el blanco	*dart board*
el dardo	*dart*

El entrenamiento
Fitness training

el aerobic	*aerobics*
la bicicleta estática	*exercise bike*
el footing; el jogging	*jogging*
las pesas	*weights*

La esgrima *Fencing*

la careta	*mask*
el florete	*foil*

La gimnasia *Gymnastics*

la cama elástica	*trampoline*
la colchoneta	*mat*
las paralelas	*parallel bars*
el potro	*horse*
el suelo	*floor*

El hockey *Hockey*

el palo	*stick*
la portería	*goal*

El snooker *Snooker*

la bola	*ball*
la mesa	*table*
el taco	*cue*

9 El ocio y los deportes *Hobbies and sports*

El tenis de mesa; el pingpong
Table tennis

la mesa	table
la pala	bat

El tiro *Shooting*

la bala	bullet
el campo de tiro	rifle range
la munición	ammunition
el rifle	rifle
el tiro al plato/	
de pichón	clay pigeon shooting

El tiro al arco *Archery*

el arco	bow
el blanco;	
la diana	target
la flecha	arrow

Los deportes aeronáuticos
Air sports

el ala delta	hang gliding
la aviación	flying
el paracaidismo	parachuting
el planeo	gliding
volar en globo	ballooning

Los deportes de montaña
Mountain sports

la escalada en rocas	rock climbing
el excursionismo a pie	mountain walking / hiking
el montañismo	mountain climbing
la orientación	orienteering
los arreos	harness

las botas de escalar	climbing boots
las clavijas de escala	pitons
la cuerda	rope
la mochila	rucksack
la piqueta	ice axe
la ropa térmica	thermal clothing
la ruta; el itinerario	route
el saco de dormir	sleeping bag
la tienda	tent

El fútbol *Football*

el campo	pitch
el club	club
el equipo	team
el partido	match
el árbitro	referee
el capitán	captain
el encargado de campo	groundsman
el entrenador	trainer
el/la espectador-a	spectator
el juez de línea	linesman
el jugador	player
la liga	league
la copa	cup
la línea	line
el poste de la portería	goal post
fuera de juego	off-side
fuera de línea	over the line
los puestos	positions
el ataque	attack
el defensa	back / defence

el delantero	*forward*
el medio	*centre*
el portero	*goalkeeper*
ganar	*to win*
empatar	*to draw*
perder	*to lose*
chutar	*to shoot*
dar un puntapié	*to kick*
fallar	*to miss*
marcar (un gol)	*to score (a goal)*
el cabezazo	*header*
el penalti	*penalty*

El equipamiento protector
Protective equipment

la codera	*elbow guard*
la rodillera	*knee guard*

El tenis *Tennis*

el adversario	*opponent*
la pareja	*partner*
el partido	*match*
el individual femenino	*ladies' singles*
el individual masculino	*men's singles*
el juego de dobles	*doubles*
los dobles mixtos	*mixed doubles*
la línea	*line*
la pelota	*ball*
la pista	*court*
la raqueta	*racket*
la red	*net*

la dejada	*let*
el servicio	*service*
cero	*love*
quince iguales	*15 all*
ventaja	*advantage*
cuarenta iguales	*deuce*
el tiebreak	*tiebreak*
juego, set y partido	*game, set and match*
servir	*to serve*
jugar	*to play*
volear	*to volley*

El golf *Golf*

la bandera	*flag*
el bunker	*bunker*
el cadi	*caddie*
el campo de golf	*golf course*
el club de golf	*golf club*
el fairway; la calle	*fairway*
el green	*green*
el hoyo	*hole*
el palo	*club*
el hierro	*iron*
la madera	*wood*
el putter	*putter*
la pelota	*ball*
el tee	*tee*

El ciclismo *Cycling*

la bicicleta de carreras	*racing bike*
la bicicleta de montaña	*mountain bike*
la bomba	*pump*
la cadena	*chain*

9 El ocio y los deportes *Hobbies and sports*

una cámara de aire de repuesto	*spare inner tube*
el ciclismo de montaña	*mountain biking*
los engranajes	*gears*
los frenos	*brakes*
el manillar	*handlebars*
los pedales	*pedals*
el pinchazo	*puncture*
los radios	*spokes*
las ruedas	*wheels*
el sillín	*saddle*
el casco	*helmet*
el maillot	*shirt*
el pantalón corto	*cycling shorts*
los guantes	*gloves*
las zapatillas	*shoes*

El atletismo *Athletics*

los bloques de salida	*blocks*
los competidores	*competitors*
el/la cronometrador-a	*timekeeper*
el estadio	*stadium*
la pista	*track*
las pruebas de campo	*field events*
el lanzamiento . . .	*throwing . . .*
de disco	*the discus*
de martillo	*the hammer*
de jabalina	*the javelin*
de peso	*(putting) the shot*

la carrera de relevos	*relay race*
el maratón	*marathon*
la marcha	*walking*
el salto	*jump*
el salto de longitud	*long jump*
el salto de altura	*high jump*
el salto con pértiga	*pole vault*
el triple salto	*triple jump*
la carrera a campo traviesa	*cross country*
el/la juez	*judge*
el/la cronometrador-a	*time keeper*
las pruebas de pista	*track events*
las vallas	*hurdles*
el biatlón	*biathlon*
la carrera	*running race*
el cronómetro	*stop watch*
la vuelta	*lap*
el pistoletazo de salida	*starting gun*

Los deportes náuticos *Water sports*

la natación	*swimming*
braza	*breast stroke*
estilo libre	*free style*
espalda	*back stroke*
mariposa	*butterfly*
el largo	*length*
el relevo	*relay*
las aletas	*flippers*

el bañador	swimming costume		la quilla	keel
las gafas	goggles		el timón	rudder
el gorro de			la vela	sail
natación	swimming hat		las vergas	spars
el tubo de				
respiración	snorkel		estribor	starboard
la crema bronceadora			babor	port
resistente	water-resistant			
al agua	sun-cream		zozobrar	capsize

el salto de	
trampolín	diving
el salto	dive
el trampolín	diving board

el submari-	
nismo	underwater diving
la botella	
de oxígeno	oxygen cylinder
el traje isotérmico	
	wet suit

El piragüismo *Canoeing*

el bote de remos	rowing boat
el chaleco	
salvavidas	life jacket
el kayac	kayak
la pala	paddle
la piragua	canoe
la popa	stern
el remo	rowing
los remos	oars
el timón	helm

La vela *Sailing*

el barco de vela	sailing boat
la caña de timón	tiller
el dingui; la lancha	
neumática	dinghy
la escota	sheet
las maromas	ropes
la orza de	
deriva	centreboard

El esquí acuático
Water skiing

la embarcación	
a motor	motor boat
fuera-borda	outboard

Los deportes de invierno
Winter sports

el esquí	skiing
el esquí alpino	alpine skiing
el esquí nórdico/	nordic/cross
de fondo	country skiing
el bastón	
de esquiar	ski stick
las botas	
de esquiar	ski boots
el descenso	downhill race
el eslálom	slalom
los esquíes	skis
la estación	
de esquí	ski resort
el mono	salopette
la pista	piste
la telesilla	ski lift

la pista de	
tobogán	toboggan run
el salto de esquí	ski jumping
el tobogán	toboggan

los patines	skates
el patinaje	
artístico	ice dance

el patinaje sobre hielo	*ice skating*	el hockey sobre hielo	*ice hockey*
la pista de patinaje	*skating rink*	los palos de hockey	*hockey sticks*
		la portería	*goal*
		el puck	*puck*

10 El cuerpo, la salud y las enfermedades
The body, health and sickness

EL CUERPO
THE BODY

Las partes del cuerpo
Parts of the body

el cuerpo	*the body*
la cara	*face*
la cabeza	*head*
la garganta	*throat*
el cuello	*neck*
el hombro	*shoulder*
el brazo	*arm*
el codo	*elbow*
la muñeca	*wrist*
el puño	*fist*
la mano	*hand*
el dedo	*finger*
el pulgar	*thumb*
el dedo anular	*ring finger*
el dedo meñique	*little finger*
el dedo índice	*index finger*
la uña	*fingernail*
el tórax	*chest*
el pecho	*bust*
la costilla	*rib*
el costado	*side*
la espalda	*back*
la cintura	*waist*
las caderas	*hips*
el pene	*penis*
los testículos	*testicles*
la pierna	*leg*
el muslo	*thigh*
la rodilla	*knee*
la pantorrilla	*calf*
el talón	*ankle*
el pie	*foot*
el talón	*heel*
la planta del pie	*sole*
el dedo del pie	*toe*
la piel	*skin*
el hueso	*bone*
la articulación	*joint*

la columna vertebral	*spine*
el esqueleto	*skeleton*
el cráneo	*skull*

Los órganos internos
Internal organs

el cerebro	*brain*
el corazón	*heart*
el cuello del útero	*cervix*
el estómago	*stomach*
el hígado	*liver*
los intestinos	*intestines*
el ligamento	*ligament*
el músculo	*muscle*
el nervio	*nerve*
la próstata	*prostrate*
los pulmones	*lungs*
los riñones	*kidneys*
la sangre	*blood*
la arteria	*artery*
el vaso sanguíneo	*blood vessel*
la vena	*vein*
el pulso	*pulse*
el sistema nervioso	*nervous system*
el tendón	*tendon*
el útero	*womb*
la vagina	*vagina*

andar	*to walk*
arrodillarse	*to kneel*
correr	*to run*
descansar	*to rest*
dormir	*to sleep*
estar de pie	*to stand*
hacer ejercicio	*to exercise*
hacer footing	*to jog*
respirar	*to breathe*
saltar	*to jump*
sentarse	*to sit*
tumbarse	*to lie down*

10 El cuerpo, la salud y las enfermedades
The body, health and sickness

LAS MOLESTIAS Y LOS DOLORES *ACHES AND PAINS*

Me duele.	*It hurts.*
Tengo dolor de ...	*I've got ...*
espalda	*backache*
oídos	*earache*
cabeza	*a headache*
muelas	*toothache*
Tengo ...	*I've got ...*
un dedo inflamado	*a sore finger*
una ampolla	*a blister*

La cara *The face*

la barbilla	*chin*	la nariz	*nose*
la boca	*mouth*	la oreja	*ear*
la ceja	*eyebrow*	el ojo	*eye*
el cutis	*complexion*	el cristalino	*lens*
los dientes	*teeth*	el iris	*iris*
la frente	*forehead*	la retina	*retina*
los labios	*lips*	el párpado	*eyelid*
la lengua	*tongue*	el pelo	*hair*
la mejilla	*cheek*	la pestaña	*eyelash*
		la piel	*skin*

Tengo ...	*I've got ...*
un grano/granos	*a spot / spots*
un forúnculo	*a boil*
una espinilla	*a blackhead*
un poro obstruido	*a blocked pore*
un oído obstruido	*a blocked ear*
cerilla en los oídos	*ear wax*
la nariz atascada	*a stuffy nose*
un catarro	*catarrh*
caspa	*dandruff*

10 El cuerpo, la salud y las enfermedades
The body, health and sickness

estornudar	*to sneeze*	sonreír	*to smile*
fruncir el ceño	*to frown*	toser	*to cough*
hacer muecas	*to grimace; make a face*		

EL ASEO Y LA COSMÉTICA
TOILETRIES AND COSMETICS

¿Tiene(-s) un-a/mi(-s) . . . ?	*Have you got a / my / some . . . ?*
bolsa de aseo	*sponge bag*
brocha de afeitar	*shaving brush*
cepillo de dientes	*toothbrush*
cepillo del pelo	*hairbrush*
cera para el vello	*leg wax*
champú	*shampoo*
compresas	*sanitary towels*
condón	*condom*
crema bronceadora	*sun cream*
crema de afeitar	*shaving cream*
crema facial	*face cream*
crema suavizante para el cabello	*conditioner*
crema/loción hidratante	*moisturiser*
cuchilla	*razor*
desodorante	*deodorant*
elixir bucal	*mouth wash*
esponja	*sponge*
jabón	*soap*
laca de uñas	*nail varnish*
lima para las uñas	*nail file*
loción para después del afeitado	*after shave*
manopla	*face cloth*
maquinilla eléctrica	*electric shaver*
pañuelo de papel	*paper handkerchief*
peine	*comb*
pinzas	*tweezers*
polvos de talco	*talcum powder*
quitaesmalte	*nail varnish remover*
secador	*hair dryer*
tampón	*tampon*
tijeras de las uñas	*nail scissors*

10 El cuerpo, la salud y las enfermedades
The body, health and sickness

cepillar	*to brush*
colocar	*to put on*
lavar	*to wash*
limpiar	*to clean*
usar	*to use*
pintarse	*to varnish*
las uñas	*one's nails*
quitarse la laca	
de uñas	*to remove varnish*

La cosmética *Cosmetics*

la brocha para	
maquillaje	*make up brush*
el colorete	*blusher*

la crema/loción desmaquilladora	
	make-up remover
el lápiz de labios	*lipstick*
el lápiz de ojos	*eye liner*
el maquillaje	*make-up*
los polvos	*face powder*
el rímel	*mascara*
la sombra	
de ojos	*eye shadow*
lavar/secar	*to wash / dry*
el pelo	*your hair*
maquillarse	*to put make up on*
desmaquillarse	*take make up off*

¡OTRA VEZ!

● *Activity:* Unscramble the anagrams.
¿Tienes mi(-s) . . . ? *Have you got my . . . ?*

banój   epien   posjean

znispa   dsareco

10 El cuerpo, la salud y las enfermedades
The body, health and sickness

LAS ENFERMEDADES
ILLNESSES

¡Que te mejores!   *Get well soon!*

la salud	*health*
en forma	*fit*
saludable	*healthy*
infeccioso-a	*infectious*
la enfermedad	*disease / illness*
la fiebre	*fever*
enfermo-a	*ill*
el mareo	*sickness*
estar mareado-a	*to feel sick*
el dolor	*pain*
la medicina	*medicine*

inflamado-a;
que duele; doloroso-a
sore; painful

Las enfermedades
Illnesses and indisposition

la acidez	*heart burn*
la anorexia	*anorexia*
la apendicitis	*appendicitis*
la apoplejía	*stroke*
la artritis	*arthritis*
el asma	*asthma*
el brazo roto	*broken arm*
la bulimia	*bulimia*
el cáncer	*cancer*
la catarata	*cataract*
la celulitis	*cellulite*
la cicatriz	*scar*
el cólera	*colera*
la conmoción	*shock*
la contusión	*bruising*
la costra	*scab*
la dermatitis	*dermatitis*
la diabetes	*diabetes*
la diarrea	*diarrhoea*
la difteria	*diptheria*

el dolor	
muscular	*muscular pain*
el eczema	*eczema*
las enfermedades	
venéreas	*venereal diseases*
el estreñimiento	*constipation*
el estrés	*stress*
la fiebre	
amarilla	*yellow fever*
la fiebre;	
la calentura	*temperature*
la gripe	*flu*
la halitosis	*halitosis*
la hemofilia	*haemophilia*
la hemorragia	*haemorrage*
las hemorroides	*haemorroides*
la hepatitis	*hepatitis*
la hernia	*hernia*
la indigestión	*indigestion*
la infección	*infection*
la malaria	*malaria*
el mareo	*travel sickness*
la meningitis	*meningitis*
la menopausia	*menopause*
la obesidad	*obesity*
las paperas	*mumps*
el picor	*itching*
el pie de atleta	*athlete's foot*
la pierna rota	*broken leg*
la polio	*polio*
la quemadura	*burn*
la quemadura	
de sol	*sunburn*
la rabia	*rabies*
el reúma	*rheumatism*
la rubéola	*German measles*
el sarampión	*measles*
el sero positivo	*HIV positive*
el SIDA	*AIDS*
la tensión	
arterial	*low / high*
alta/baja	*blood pressure*
el tétano	*tetanus*

10 El cuerpo, la salud y las enfermedades
The body, health and sickness

la tuberculosis	*tuberculosis*	el miembro	
la varicela	*chicken pox*	artificial	*artificial limb*
		la enfermedad	
la bacteria	*bacteria*	crónica	*chronic illness*
la infección	*infection*	la enfermedad	
el virus	*virus*	intermitente	*spasmodic illness*
ciego-a	*blind*	la enfermera	*nurse*
cojo-a	*lame*	el/la	
minusválido-a	*handicapped*	fisioterapeuta	*physiotherapist*
mudo-a	*dumb*	el/la médico	*doctor*
parapléjico-a	*paraplegic*	el/la óptico	*optician*
sordo-a	*deaf*	el/la osteópata	*osteopath*
		el/la podólogo-a	*chiropodist*
la silla			
de ruedas	*wheel chair*	un ambulatorio	*surgery*
		una cita	*appointment*

10 El cuerpo, la salud y las enfermedades
The body, health and sickness

EN EL MÉDICO *AT THE DOCTORS*

¿Puedo concertar una cita?	*Can I make an appointment?*
Me siento mal/enfermo-a.	*I feel ill.*
Me siento mareado-a.	*I feel sick.*
Tengo . . .	*I have . . .*
dolor de estómago	*stomach ache*
dolor de garganta	*a sore throat*
fiebre	*a temperature*
un resfriado	*a cold*
tos	*a cough*
¿Puede darme algo para . . . ?	*Can I have something for . . . ?*
el dolor de cabeza	*a headache*
enviar al especialista	*to refer to a consultant*
hacerse un análisis	*to have an analysis done*
recetar un tratamiento	*to prescribe treatment*
recetar medicación	*to prescribe medication*
tomar la tensión arterial	*to take ones blood pressure*
tomar una muestra	*to take a sample*
tomarse la temperatura	*to take ones temperature*
tomarse el pulso	*to take ones pulse*

EN EL DENTISTA
AT THE DENTIST

la clínica dental	*dental surgery*
el/la dentista	*dentist*
la enfermera dental	*dental nurse*
la encía	*gum*
el diente; la muela	*tooth*
la raíz	*root*
el colmillo	*canine*
el diente de leche	*milk tooth*
los dientes postizos; la dentadura postiza	*false teeth; dentures*
el empaste	*filling*
el incisivo	*incisor*
la mandíbula superior/inferior	*upper / lower jaw*
el molar	*molar*
la muela del juicio	*wisdom tooth*
el (aparato) corrector	*brace*

10 El cuerpo, la salud y las enfermedades
The body, health and sickness

Tengo . . .	*I have . . .*
dolor de muelas	*toothache*
un absceso	*an abscess*
Se me ha caído/roto . . .	*I have lost / broken . . .*
un diente	*a tooth*
un empaste	*a filling*
una funda	*a cap*
un puente	*a bridge*

el cepillo		la pasta	
de dientes	*toothbrush*	dentífrica	*toothpaste*
la seda dental		el palillo	
	dental floss	de dientes	*tooth pick*

LOS TRATAMIENTOS Y LAS CURAS
TREATMENT AND REMEDIES

Los primeros auxilios
First aid

los apósitos adhesivos;	
las tiritas	*sticking plaster*
el botiquín	*medicine cabinet*
el cabestrillo	*sling*
la escayola	*plaster / cast*
la gasa	*lint*
el imperdible	*safety pin*
las pinzas	*tweezers*
las tijeras	*scissors*
la venda	*bandage*
el corte	*cut*
el hematoma	*bruise*
la herida	*wound*
la quemadura	*burn*

Los medicamentos
Medicines

el antibiótico	*antibiotic*
los comprimidos	*tablets*
los comprimidos . . .	
	. . . tablets
antiinflamatorios	
	anti-inflammatory
contra la malaria	
	anti-malaria
la crema	*cream*
la crema	
antiséptica	*antiseptic cream*
la crema anti-	*anti-histamine*
histamínica	*cream*
las gotas	*drops*
las infusiones	*infusions*
el inhalador	*inhaler*
las pastillas	*lozenges*
la píldora	*the Pill*
las píldoras	*pills*

10 El cuerpo, la salud y las enfermedades
The body, health and sickness

los somníferos — *sleeping pills*
los supositorios — *suppository*
los tranquilizantes — *tranquillizers*
el vendaje — *dressing*

Otros remedios
Other remedies

la medicina alternativa — *alternative medicine*
la acupuntura — *acupuncture*
la aromaterapia — *aromatherapy*
la fisioterapia — *physiotherapy*
la homeopatía — *homeopathy*
la reflexología — *reflexology*

EL HOSPITAL
HOSPITAL

la ambulancia — *ambulance*
la clínica; el centro médico; el ambulatorio — *clinic*

el/la cirujano — *surgeon*
el/la especialista — *consultant*
el/la ginecólogo — *gynaecologist*
el/la ortodoncista — *orthodontist*
el/la pediatra — *paediatrician*

el/la médico — *doctor*
la enfermera — *nurse*
el/la paciente — *patient*

la cama — *bed*
la camilla — *stretcher*
la sala — *ward*

la dieta — *diet*
la fibra dietética — *dietary fibre*
seguir una dieta equilibrada — *follow a healthy diet*

adelgazar/ engordar — *to lose / gain weight*
ayunar — *to fast*
hacer ejercicio — *to exercise*

atragantarse — *to choke*
desmayarse; perder el sentido — *to faint*
esterilizar — *to sterilise*
infectar — *to infect*
padecer — *to suffer*

el/la anestesista — *anaesthetist*
la anestesia local/general — *local / general anaesthetic*
la cirugía — *surgery*
el escalpelo — *scalpel*
el goteo — *drip*
el instrumental — *instruments*
el láser — *laser*
la medicina intravenosa — *intravenous medicine*
la operación — *operation*
el quirófano — *operating theatre*
la radiografía — *an x-ray*

la convalecencia — *convalescence*
la recuperación — *recuperation*

convalecer — *to convalesce*
doler — *to hurt*
escayolar — *to plaster*
inocular — *to inoculate*
mejorar — *to improve*
operar — *to operate*
sentirse bien — *to feel well*

10 El cuerpo, la salud y las enfermedades
The body, health and sickness

sentirse
  mal/enfermo-a *to feel ill*

tener náuseas;
  vomitar   *to be sick; vomit*
vacunar   *to vaccinate*

EL TABACO, LAS DROGAS Y EL ALCOHOL
SMOKING, DRUGS AND ALCOHOL

Prohibido fumar   *No smoking*

El/la fumador-a/no fumador-a
Smoker/non-smoker

el alquitrán	*tar*
el cenicero	*ashtray*
las cerillas	*matches*
los cigarrillos	*cigarettes*
los cigarros puros;	
habanos	*cigars*
el mechero	*lighter*
la nicotina	*nicotine*
el papel	
de fumar	*cigarette paper*
la pipa	*pipe*
el tabaco	*tobacco*
el cáncer	*cancer*
el enfisema	*emphysema*
fumar	*to smoke*
dejar de fumar	*to give up smoking*
fumar menos	*to cut down*
	on smoking
inhalar; aspirar	
el humo	*to inhale*

Las drogas *Drugs*

el cannabis	*cannabis*
el hachís	*hashish*
la marihuana	*marijuana*
la cocaína	*cocaine*
el crack	*crack*
la heroína	*heroin*
el éxtasis	*ecstasy*
las anfetaminas	*amphetamines*
las drogas	
blandas	*soft drugs*
las drogas duras	*hard drugs*
las drogas de	
diseño	*designer drugs*
inyectarse	*to inject*
la aguja	*needle*
la jeringuilla	*syringe*
la drogadicción	*drug addiction*
el síndrome de	*withdrawal*
la abstinencia	*symptoms*
el mono	*cold turkey*
el/la drogadicto-a	*drug addict*
la toxicomanía	*drug abuse*

10 El cuerpo, la salud y las enfermedades
The body, health and sickness

El alcohol *Alcohol*

El/ella bebe demasiado.	*He/she drinks too much.*	dejar de beber	*to give up drinking*
desalcoholizarse	*to dry out*	el/la abstemio-a	*teetotaller*
		el/la alcohólico-a	*alcoholic*

Si bebes no conduzcas	*Don't drink and drive*

11 Las instituciones *Institutions*

LA BANCA Y LA BOLSA
BANKING AND FINANCE

El dinero y el banco
Money and the bank

el banco	*bank*
la caja de ahorros	*savings bank*
la sociedad de préstamo inmobiliario	*building society*
la sucursal	*branch*
el billete	*banknote*
la caja	*till*
el/la cajero-a	*cashier*
el cajero automático	*cash machine*
el cambio	*change*
el cambio de divisa	*currency rates*
el cheque; el talón	*cheque*
la comisión (por servicio bancario)	*commission*
el crédito	*credit*
la cuenta bancaria	*bank account*
la cuenta corriente	*current account*
la cuenta de ahorros	*savings account*
el débito	*debit*
el depósito	*deposit*
el dinero	*money*
las divisas	*foreign currency*
en números rojos	*in the red*
el estado de cuenta	*statement*
la firma	*signature*

la hipoteca	*mortgage*
la identificación	*identification*
la letra bancaria	*banker's draft*
la libra esterlina	*pound*
la libreta de ahorros	*savings book*
la moneda	*currency*
el número de sucursal bancaria	*bank sort code*
el préstamo	*loan*
la retirada de fondos de un banco	*withdrawal*
el saldo	*balance*
el saldo deudor	*overdraft*
la tarjeta de crédito	*credit card*
la tarjeta de identidad bancaria	*cheque card*
la transferencia bancaria	*transfer*
el billete falsificado	*forged note*
el cheque abierto	*open cheque*
el cheque al portador	*cheque payable to the bearer*
el cheque cruzado	*crossed cheque*
el cheque de viaje	*traveller's cheque*
el cheque en blanco	*blank cheque*
el cheque nulo	*invalid cheque*
la falsificación	*forgery*
cambiar dinero	*to change money*
cobrar un cheque	*to cash a cheque*
depositar	*to deposit*
devolver; reintegrar	*to pay back; repay*

falsificar	*to forge*
ingresar	*to pay in*
prestar	*to lend*
tomar prestado	*to borrow*

La bolsa *Stock Exchange*

la acción	*share*
el activo	*asset*
el beneficio	*profit*
el capital	*capital*
el certificado	*certificate*
la compra	*purchase*
el coste de vida	*cost of living*
la depreciación	*depreciation*
la deuda	*debt*
los gastos	*expenses*
el índice	*index*
la inflación	*inflation*
el interés	*interest*
el inventario; el capital comercial	*stock*
la inversión	*investment*
el pago	*payment*
el porcentaje	*percentage*
el préstamo	*loan*
el presupuesto	*budget*
el recibo	*receipt*
la suma; la cantidad	*sum*
el valor	*value*
la venta	*sale*
el mercado bajista	*bear market*
el mercado alcista	*bull market*

Los valores
Stocks and shares

alimentación	*food*
banca	*banking*
comunicaciones	*communications*
construcción	*construction*
electricidad	*electricity*
inversión	*investment*
químicas	*chemicals*
sidero-metalúrgicas	*mining*

la desgravación fiscal	*tax allowances*
el impuesto	*tax*
el impuesto sobre la renta	*income tax*
el interés	*interest*
el IVA	*VAT*

Las divisas *Currencies*

el mercado de divisas	*currency market*
el billete	*note*
la moneda	*coin*
el/la comprador-a	*buyer*
el/la vendedor-a	*seller*
el dólar EE.UU	*American dollar*
el dólar australiano	*Australian dollar*
el franco francés/suizo	*French / Swiss franc*
la libra esterlina	*pound sterling*
la lira	*lire*
el marco alemán	*Deutschmark*
la peseta	*peseta*
el yen	*yen*
ahorrar	*to save*
cobrar intereses	*to charge interest*

comprar	to buy	prestar	to lend
costar	to cost	tomar prestado	to borrow
gastar	to spend	valer	to be worth
invertir	to invest	vender	to sell
pagar	to pay		
pagar impuestos	to pay tax	barato-a	cheap
perder	to lose	costoso-a; caro-a	dear; expensive

LA IGLESIA Y LA RELIGIÓN   *CHURCH AND RELIGION*

la religión	religion	el Hinduismo	Hinduism
		el Islamismo	Islam
el Budismo	Buddhism	el Judaísmo	Judaism
el Catolicismo	Catholicism		
el Cristianismo	Christianity		

Soy...	I am...
ateo-a	an atheist
agnóstico-a	an agnostic
budista	a Buddhist
católico-a	a Catholic
cristiano-a	a Christian
cuáquero-a	a Quaker
hinduista	a Hindu
judío-a	a Jew
musulmán-ana	a Moslem
testigo de Jehová	a Jehovah's witness

Alá	Allah	el cardenal	cardinal
Buda	Buddha	el/la discípulo-a	disciple
Cristo	Christ	el imán	imam
Dios	God	el mártir	martyr
el Espíritu		el mesías	messiah
Santo	Holy Ghost	la monja	nun
Mahoma	Mohammed	el monje	monk
Moisés	Moses	el obispo	bishop
la Virgen María	the Virgin Mary	el Papa	the Pope
		el pastor	minister
el apóstol	apostle	el/la pecador-a	sinner
el arzobispo	archbishop	el/la peregrino-a	pilgrim

el profeta	prophet	el ángel	angel
el rabino	rabbi	el demonio	devil
el sacerdote	priest		
el/la santo-a	saint	el cielo	heaven
el vicario	vicar	la condenación	damnation
		el infierno	hell
la bendición	blessing	el nirvana	Nirvana
la comunión	communion	el paraíso	paradise
el culto; el oficio		el purgatorio	purgatory
religioso	service	la salvación	salvation
el himno	hymn		
la misa	mass	la creencia	belief
el motete	anthem	la creación	creation
la oración;		la fe	faith
el rezo	prayer	la guerra santa	Holy war
el salmo	psalm	el milagro	miracle
el sermón	sermon	la peregrinación	pilgrimage
la aguja	spire	absolver	to absolve
el altar	altar	arrepentirse	to repent
la capilla	chapel	cantar	to sing; chant
la catedral	cathedral	confesarse	to confess
el coro	choir	convertir/-se	to convert
la cúpula	cupola	creer/no creer	to believe /
la iglesia	church		not believe
la mezquita	mosque	ir a la iglesia;	
la nave	nave	asistir al culto	to attend church
la sinagoga	synagogue	ir/asistir a misa	to go to Mass
el templo	temple	ir en	to make a
		peregrinación	pilgrimage
la cruz	cross	meditar	to meditate
la vela	candle	orar; rezar	to pray
		predicar	to preach
		venerar; adorar	to worship

11 Las instituciones *Institutions*

LA EDUCACIÓN
EDUCATION

La escuela; el colegio
School

el jardín de infancia	*kindergarten*
la guardería	*play school*
la escuela primaria	*primary school*
la escuela secundaria; el instituto	*secondary school*
el colegio privado	*private school*
el colegio público	*state school*
la universidad laboral	*technical college*
el politécnico	*polytechnic*
la universidad	*university*
el/la alumno-a	*pupil*
el/la estudiante	*student*
el/la director-a	*headmaster / mistress*
el/la subdirector-a	*deputy*
el/la profesor-a	*teacher*
el/la bibliotecario-a	*librarian*
el/la celador-a/ portero-a	*caretaker*
el/la secretario-a	*school secretary*
la clase	*class*
la lección	*lesson*
el recreo	*break*
la matrícula	*registration*

Las asignaturas *Subjects*

el alemán	*German*
el arte	*Art*
la biología	*Biology*
las ciencias	*Science*
la educación física	*P.E.*
el español	*Spanish*
la física	*Physics*
el francés	*French*
la geografía	*Geography*
la historia	*History*
la informática	*I.T.*
el inglés	*English*
las matemáticas	*Mathematics*
la música	*Music*
la química	*Chemistry*
la sociología	*Sociology*
la tecnología	*Technology*
la calificación; la nota; la evaluación	*mark; grade*
la composición	*essay*
la conducta	*behaviour*
los deberes	*homework*
el ejercicio	*exercise*
la escritura	*writing*
el examen	*examination*
el examen escrito	*written examination*
el examen oral	*oral examination*
el informe	*report*
la lectura	*reading*
la ortografía	*spelling*
la puntuación	*punctuation**
el trabajo escrito	*written work*

(* See also *Arts and the Media*, page 103)

11 Las instituciones *Institutions*

aprender	*to learn*
estudiar	*to study*
repasar	*to revise*

presentarse a	
un examen	*to sit an exam*
aprobar	
un examen	*to pass an exam*
suspender	
un examen	*to fail an exam*
volver a presentarse	
a un examen	*to re-sit an exam*

el certificado;	
el diploma	*certificate*
el título	*qualification*
la licenciatura	*degree*
el/la graduado-a;	
el/la bachiller	*graduate*
el/la licenciado-a	*bachelor*
el doctorado	*doctorate*
el máster	*master's degree*
la tesis doctoral	*thesis*

el/la profesor-a	
universitario-a	
	lecturer
el/la catedrático-a	
	professor
el/la doctor-a	*doctor*

Los estudios universitarios
University subjects

la arqueología	*Archeology*
las ciencias	*Sciences*
el derecho	*Law*
la electrónica	*Electronics*

la filosofía	*Philosphy*
la historia	*History*
la informática	*Information Technology*
la ingeniería	*Engineering*
las lenguas clásicas	*Classical Languages*
las lenguas modernas	*Modern Languages*
las letras; las humanidades	*Humanities*
la medicina	*Medicine*
el periodismo	*Journalism*
la psicología	*Psychology*
la psiquiatría	*Psychiatry*
la sociología	*Sociology*

el paraninfo	*lecture theatre*
el seminario	*seminar room*

el/la candidato-a	*candidate*
el/la examinador-a	
	examiner
el aprobado	*pass mark*
el examen	*exam paper*
la pregunta	*question*
la respuesta	*answer*
el resultado	*result*

el año académico;	
el curso	*school year*
el día libre	*day off*
la emergencia	*emergency*
el nuevo año académico;	
el nuevo curso	*new school year*
el semestre	*semester*
el trimestre	*term*
las vacaciones	*holidays*

11 Las instituciones *Institutions*

EL ORDEN PÚBLICO
LAW AND ORDER

El crimen y la policía
Crime and the police

la agresión	*assault*
la alarma antirrobo	*burglar alarm*
el arma	*weapon*
el arma de fuego	*gun; firearm*
el/la asesino-a	*murderer*
el ataque	*attack*
la agresión sexual	*sexual attack*
el atentado contra el pudor/la moral	*indecent assault*
el atraco	*hold-up*
el camello; el traficante	*drug dealer*
el carterista	*pickpocket*
el casco	*helmet*
el cazador furtivo	*poacher*
el chantaje	*blackmail*
el coche-patrulla	*police car*
el/la cómplice	*accomplice*
con violencia	*with violence*
el crimen; el delito	*crime*
el criminal	*criminal*
la detención	*arrest*
la emergencia	*emergency*
el/la espía	*spy*
la falsificación	*forgery*
forzar una entrada	*break in*
el fraude	*fraud*
el/la gamberro-a	*hooligan; yob*
el/la guerrillero-a	*guerrilla*
el hurto	*shoplifting*
el incendio provocado	*arson*
el/la ladrón-a	*thief; burglar*
la multa	*fine*
los narcóticos	*narcotics*
el narcotraficante	*drug dealer*
el narcotráfico	*drugs traffic*
la pandilla	*gang*
la pelea	*fight*
el perista	*receiver; fence*
la pistola	*pistola*
el/la provocador-a de incendio	*arsonist*
el/la rehén	*hostage*
el rescate	*rescue*
el revólver	*revolver*
el robo	*robbery*
el secuestro	*kidnapping*
el secuestro aéreo	*hijacking*
el sistema de seguridad	*security system*
los teléfonos de urgencia	*emergency telephone numbers*
el/la terrorista	*terrorist*
el/la traidor	*traitor*
el/la policía	*police officer*
el uniforme	*uniform*
la urgencia	*emergency*
el veneno	*poison*
amenazar	*to threaten*
apuñalar	*to stab*
asesinar	*to murder*
atacar	*to attack*
atracar	*to hold up*
buscar	*to search*
disparar	*to shoot*
engañar	*to deceive*
espiar	*to spy*
hacer trampas	*to cheat*
matar	*to kill*
pegar	*to mug*
procesar	*to prosecute*
robar	*to burgle; rob*
violar	*to rape*

11 Las instituciones *Institutions*

Ante los tribunales *In court*

el/la abogado	*lawyer*
la absolución	*acquittal*
el acta	*act*
la apelación	*appeal*
el banquillo (de los acusados)	*dock*
los cargos	*charges*
el caso	*case*
la celda	*cell*
la condena a perpetuidad	*life sentence*
la culpabilidad	*guilt*
culpable	*guilty*
los daños	*damages*
el delito menor	*minor offence*
la demanda	*complaint*
el/la detenido-a; el/la acusado-a	*prisoner*
el fallo provisional	*decree nisi*
la fianza	*bail*
inocente	*innocent*
el interrogatorio	*interrogation*
el/la juez	*judge*

el juicio	*prosecution*
el jurado	*jury*
el juramento	*oath*
la ley	*law*
la libertad bajo fianza	*release on bail*
la libertad condicional	*probation*
la multa	*fine*
la ofensa	*offence*
la orden judicial	*warrant*
la prisión	*prison*
el secretario	*clerk of the court*
la sentencia	*sentence*
el tribunal de justicia	*law court*
el veredicto	*verdict*
confesar	*confess*
declararse culpable	*to plead guilty*
declararse inocente	*to plead innocent*
jurar	*to swear*
ser testigo	*to witness*

11 Las instituciones *Institutions*

EL EJÉRCITO
THE MILITARY

Las Fuerzas Armadas
The Armed Forces

la guerra	*war*
declarar	
la guerra	*to declare war*
la paz	*peace*
firmar un	*to sign a peace*
tratado de paz	*treaty*
el acuerdo	*agreement*
el aliado	*ally*
el alto el fuego	*ceasefire*
la amenaza	*threat*
el asalto	*assault*
el ataque	*attack*
la batalla	*battle*
el bloqueo	*blockade*
el enemigo	*enemy*
las fuerzas de	
pacificación	*peacekeeping*
	troops
el golpe	*coup*
la Guerra Fría	*Cold War*
la rendición	*surrender*
el repliegue	*withdrawal*
la retirada	*retreat*
las sanciones	*sanctions*
el/la terrorista	*terrorist*
las tropas de las	*United Nations*
Naciones Unidas	*forces*
el casco	*helmet*
el vehículo	*vehicle*
la vigilancia	*surveillance*

El ejército de tierra *The army*

la artillería	*artillery*
el campamento	*camp*

el capitán general	
del ejército	*field marshall*
la comandancia	*command*
la compañía	*company*
el coronel	*colonel*
el cuartel	*barracks*
el cuartel	
general	*HQ*
el general	*general*
la infantería	*infantry*
la ley marcial	*court martial*
el lugarteniente	*lieutenant*
el objetor de	*conscientious*
conciencia	*objector*
el oficial	*officer*
el sargento	*sergeant*
el servicio militar;	
la mili	*military service*
el centinela	*sentry*
la graduación	*rank*
la patrulla	*patrol*
el recluta	*recruit*
el soldado	*soldier; private*
el tanque	*tank*
el transporte	
de tropas	*personnel carrier*
las tropas	*troops*

La marina *The navy*

el almirante	*admiral*
el astillero	
naval	*naval dockyard*
el buque de	
guerra	*battleship*
el capitán	*captain*
el crucero	*cruiser*
la flota	*fleet*
la fragata	*frigate*
el marinero	*sailor*
el piloto	*pilot*
el portaaviones	*aircraft carrier*

el submarino	*submarine*
la tripulación	*crew*
el vigía	*watch*

La aviación *The air force*

el aviador	*airman*
el avión	
a reacción	*jet*
la base aérea	*air force base*
el caza	*fighter (plane)*
el copiloto	*co-pilot*
el escuadrón	*squadron*
el helicóptero	*helicopter*
el manteni-	
miento	*maintenance*
el navegante	*navigator*
el piloto	*pilot*
el radar	*radar*

Las armas *Weapons*

la ametralla-	
dora	*machine gun*
el arma de	
fuego	*gun*

las armas	
químicas	*chemical weapons*
las armas	
nucleares	*nuclear weapons*
la bomba	*bomb*
la granada	
de mano	*hand grenade*
la mina	*mine*
el misil	*missile*
el misil de crucero	
	cruise missile
el misil	
teledirigido	*guided missile*
el mortero	*mortar*
el objetivo	*target*
el proyectil	*shell*
el revólver	*revolver*
el rifle	*rifle*
el torpedo	*torpedo*
bombardear	*to bomb*
defender	*to defend*
disparar	*to shoot*
luchar	*to fight*
navegar	*to sail*
volar	*to fly*

11 Las instituciones *Institutions*

LA POLÍTICA Y EL GOBIERNO
POLITICS AND GOVERNMENT

El gobierno municipal
Local government

la alcaldía	*town council*
el alcalde	*mayor*
la alcaldesa	*mayoress*
asuntos sociales	*social services*
el ayuntamiento	*town hall*
los concejales	*town councillors*
la contribución municipal	*rates*
la corporación municipal	*elected representatives*
el jefe del ejecutivo	*chief executive*

la junta municipal	*council meeting*
los impuestos municipales	*local taxes*
la oficina de empleo	*employment office*

El gobierno nacional
National government

el Congreso de los Diputados	*House of Commons*
los Cortes	*Parliament*
el/la diputado-a	*member of parliament*
el Senado	*Senate*
el distrito electoral	*constituency*
la economía	*economy*
la elección	*election*
el escaño	*seat of parliament*
el gobierno	*government*

el Ministerio de ...	*Ministry of ...*
el/la ministro-a de ...	*Minister of ...*
Agricultura, Pesca y Alimentación	*Agriculture, Fisheries and Food*
Asuntos Sociales	*Social Affairs*
Cultura	*Heritage*
Defensa	*Defence*
Educación y Ciencia	*Education and Science*
Empleo y Seguridad Social	*Employment*
Hacienda y Economía	*Finance*
Interior	*Home Office*
Obras Públicas, Transportes y Medio Ambiente	*Transport and Environment*
Salud y Consumo	*Health and Safety*

el partido	*party*
el/la político-a	*politician*
el/la presidente	*president*
el/la presidente del gobierno	*prime minister*
el cónsul	*consul*

el diplomático	*diplomat*
la embajada	*embassy*
el/la embajador-a	*ambassador*
el/la enviado-a	*envoy*

141

11 **Las instituciones** *Institutions*

someter a			tomar la	
debate	*to debate*		palabra	*to speak*
sondear	*to canvass*		votar	*to vote*

12 La ciudad y las compras *Town and shopping*

la ciudad	*town / city*
la ciudad de interés histórico	*historical town*

EL CENTRO
THE TOWN CENTRE

el aparcamiento	*car park*
el ayuntamiento	*town hall*
el banco	*bank*
el bar	*bar*
la biblioteca	*library*
el café	*cafe*
el cine	*cinema*
la comisaría	*police station*
Correos	*post office*
la estación	*station*
la estación de autobuses/trenes	*bus / train station*
el estadio de fútbol	*football stadium*
el hotel	*hotel*
el jardín botánico	*botanical gardens*
el mercado	*market*
el museo	*museum*
el museo de pinturas	*art gallery*
la oficina de turismo	*tourist office*
la oficina del ayuntamiento	*council office*
el parque	*park*
la piscina	*swimming pool*
la plaza de toros	*bull ring*

la ciudad industrial	*industrial town*
el puerto	*port*

la plaza del mercado	*market place*
el polideportivo	*leisure centre*
el restaurante	*restaurant*
la sala de conciertos	*concert hall*
la sociedad inmobiliaria	*estate agent*
el teatro	*theatre*
el zoo	*zoo*

la acera	*pavement*
la avenida	*avenue*
la calle	*street*
la calzada	*middle of the road*
la carretera	*road*
el carril para ciclistas	*bicycle track*
el cruce	*intersection*
la glorieta	*roundabout*
la indicación; la señal	*sign post*
la parada de autobuses	*bus stop*
el paso de cebra	*pedestrian crossing*
el paso elevado	*level crossing*
el paso subterráneo	*subway*
el semáforo	*traffic lights*
la zona peatonal	*pedestrian area*

12 La ciudad y las compras *Town and shopping*

LAS TIENDAS Y LAS COMPRAS
SHOPS AND SHOPPING

la agencia de viajes	*travel agent*
la carnicería	*butchers*
la confitería	*sweet shop*
el estanco	*tobacconist*
la farmacia	*chemist*
la ferretería; la droguería	*ironmongers*
la floristería	*flower shop*
la tienda de fotografía	*photographers*
la gasolinera	*petrol station*
los grandes almacenes	*department store*
la panadería	*bakery*
la papelería	*stationers*
la pastelería	*cake shop*
la peluquería	*hairdressers*
la pescadería	*fish shop*
el quiosco	*newsagents*
la tienda de comestibles	*grocers*
la tienda de modas	*clothes shop*
la tintorería	*dry cleaners*
la verdulería; la frutería	*greengrocers*
la zapatería	*shoe shop*
junto a	*next door to*
enfrente (del cine)	*opposite (the cinema)*
en la primera/ siguiente calle ...	*in the first / next street ...*
a la izquierda/ derecha	*on the left / right*
después del semáforo	*after the lights*
cruzando la calle	*across the road*
en la plaza del mercado	*in the marketplace*
en la plaza	*in the square*
en la carretera/ calle	*in the road / street*
allí	*over there*
al volver la esquina	*around the corner*
al otro lado de la calle	*on the other side of the road*

De compras *Shopping*

¿Tiene ...?	*Have you got ...?*
Quisiera ...	*I would like ...*
una botella de ...	*a bottle of ...*
un frasco de ...	*a jar of ...*
una caja de ...	*a box of ...*
un paquete de ...	*a packet of ...*
un tubo de ...	*a tube of ...*
un estuche de ...	*a case of ...*
un bidón de ...	*a drum of ...*
una lata de ...	*a can / tin of ...*
un sobre de ...	*a sachet of ...*

12 La ciudad y las compras *Town and shopping*

al natural — *fresh*
enlatado-a — *tinned*
crudo-a — *raw*
cocido-a — *cooked*

¿Cuánto? — *How much?*
un kilo — *a kilo*
medio kilo — *half a kilo*
un litro — *a litre*
medio litro — *half a litre*

¿Cuánto cuesta? — *How much does it cost?*
Eso es todo. — *That's all.*
Gracias. — *Thank you.*
Lo siento, no tengo cambio. — *I'm sorry I haven't any change.*

En los grandes almacenes
In the department store

Planta sótano — *Basement*

Supermercado — *Food Hall*
Menaje-Hogar — *Kitchenware*
Bricolaje — *DIY*

Planta baja — *Ground floor*

Artículos de Piel — *Leather goods*
Papelería — *Stationery*
Música y Radio/ Sonido — *Music and Radio*
Agencia de Viajes — *Travel agents*
Cafetería — *Snack bar*
Perfumería — *Perfumery*
Cosmética — *Cosmetics*
Ropa de Caballero — *Gentlemen's clothing*
Fotografía — *Photography*

Primera planta — *First floor*

Moda — *Fashion*
Lencería; Ropa Interior — *Underwear*
Vestidos — *Dresses*
Trajes — *Suits*
Coordinados — *Separates*
Ropa Deportiva — *Casual wear*
Trajes de Noche — *Evening wear*

Segunda planta — *Second floor*

Ropa de Cama — *Bed linen*
Ropa de Casa — *Household linens*
Porcelana y Cristal — *China and glassware*
Cuberterías — *Cutlery*
Deportes — *Sports and sportswear*
Moda Infantil y Juguetería — *Childrenswear and Toys*

Tercera planta — *Third floor*

Muebles — *Furniture*
Alfombras; Moquetas — *Carpeting*
Cortinas; Coordinados — *Home furnishings*
Electro-domésticos — *Electrical goods*
Ordenadores; Electrónica — *Computers*
Televisión y Vídeos; Imagen — *Television and videos*

Cuarta planta — *Fourth floor*

Restaurante — *Restaurant*
Servicio de atención al cliente — *Customer services*
Servicios; Lavabos — *Toilets*
Oficinas — *Offices*

12 La ciudad y las compras *Town and shopping*

¿Dónde está . . . ?	*Where is the . . . ?*
el ascensor	*lift*
el departamento de . . .	*. . . department*
la escalera mecánica	*escalator*
el mostrador	*counter*
la salida	*exit*
¿Dónde están los probadores?	*Where are the changing rooms?*

Comprando
Making purchases

¿Cuánto es?	*How much is it?*	demasiado grande/	
Es demasiado.	*It's too much.*	pequeño-a	*too big / small*
demasiado		Está	
caro-a	*too expensive*	estropeado-a.	*It's damaged.*

¿Tiene algo . . .	*Have you got anything . . .*
más barato-a?	*cheaper?*
más caro-a?	*more expensive?*
más grande?	*bigger?*
mejor?	*better?*
en (rojo)?	*in (red)?*
¿De dónde es/son?	*Where is it / are they from?*
¿De qué es/son?	*What is it / are they made of?*
¿Puedo probármelo?	*Can I try it on?*
¿Tiene . . .	*Have you got . . .*
una talla más grande/pequeña?	*a size bigger / smaller?*
algo más ancho/estrecho	*something wider / narrower?*
algo más largo/corto?	*something longer / shorter*
(No) me gusta.	*I like / don't like it.*
(No) me está bien.	*It fits / doesn't fit.*
(No) me sienta bien.	*It suits me / doesn't suit me.*
El color/estilo (no) me sienta bien.	*The colour / style suits (doesn't suit) me.*

Me lo/la llevo.	*I'll take it.*
¿Puedo encargar un-a . . . ?	*Can I order a . . . ?*
¿Dónde hay que pagar?	*Where do I pay?*
¿Aceptan tarjetas de crédito?	*Do you take credit cards?*
¿Aceptan un cheque?	*Do you take a cheque?*
No tengo cambio.	*I haven't any change.*
¿A qué hora se abre/cierra?	*What time do you open / close?*
¿Pueden mandarlo a mi hotel?	*Can you send it to my hotel?*
¿Cuándo estará listo?	*When will it be ready?*
¿Pueden arreglar (mi reloj)?	*Can you repair (my watch)*

EN LA PELUQUERÍA
AT THE HAIRDRESSERS

la cola de	
caballo	*pony tail*
el flequillo	*fringe*
el moldeador	*wave*
el pelo/el cabello	*hair*
la peluca	*wig*
la permanente	*perm*
el postizo	*hair piece*
la trenza	*plait*
corto/largo	*short / long*
ondulado/rizado	*wavy / curly*
lacio; liso	*straight*
con brillo	*shiny*

el acondicionador	
	conditioner
el champú	*shampoo*
la navaja	*razor*
las tijeras	*scissors*
cortar	*to cut*
cortar las	
puntas	*to trim*
decolorar	*to bleach*
lavar	*to wash*
marcar	*to set*
rizar	*to curl*
secar con secador	
de mano	*to blow dry*
teñir	*to dye*

12 La ciudad y las compras *Town and shopping*

EN EL BANCO Y EN CORREOS
AT THE BANK AND POST OFFICE

El banco *Bank*

la caja	*cash desk*
el cajero	*cashier*
el cambio	*money exchange*
el departamento de extranjero	*foreign transactions*
la cola	*queue*
la hoja	*form*
el horario	*opening hours*
la ventanilla	*counter*
los billetes	*notes*
el cheque	*cheque*
la divisa	*currency*
el giro postal internacional	*international money order*
en metálico	*in cash*
las monedas	*coins*
el talonario de cheques	*cheque book*
la tarjeta de crédito	*credit card*

Cambiar dinero *Changing money*

Quisiera cobrar un cheque de viaje.	*I would like to cash a traveller's cheque.*
Quisiera cambiar dinero.	*I would like to change some money.*
¿Qué tengo que hacer?	*What do I have to do?*
¿Dónde tengo que ir?	*Where do I have to go?*
¿Dónde hay que firmar?	*Where do I sign?*
¿Dónde puedo cobrar el dinero?	*Where do I get my cash?*
Aquí tiene mi pasaporte/carnet de identidad.	*Here is my passport / identity card.*
¿Cómo funciona el cajero automático?	*How do I operate the cash machine?*
Mi número de identificación personal es . . .	*My PIN number is . . .*
¿Cuánto me dan por . . . ?	*How much do I get for . . . ?*
¿Cuál es el tipo de cambio?	*What is the exchange rate?*
¿Cuánto tengo en mi cuenta?	*How much have I got in my account?*
Quiero sacar dinero.	*I want to withdraw some money.*
Mi nombre/clave es . . .	*My name / code word is . . .*
¿Cuál es mi saldo actual?	*What is my current balance?*
He perdido mi . . .	*I have lost my . . .*
tarjeta de crédito	*credit card*
talonario de cheques	*cheque book*
dinero	*money*

12 La ciudad y las compras *Town and shopping*

cambiar dinero	*to change money*
cobrar un	
cheque	*to cash a cheque*
firmar	*to sign*
sacar/retirar	
dinero	*to withdraw money*

Correos *Post office*

la carta	*letter*
el giro postal	*postal order*
el mostrador	*counter*
el paquete	*parcel*
el sello	*stamp*
el sobre	*envelope*
la tarjeta postal	*postcard*
el telegrama	*telegram*
la ventanilla	*position*

El teléfono *Telephone*

(See *The Company*, page 97 for
further telephone vocabulary.)

el aparato;	
el auricular	*handset*
la cabina	
de teléfono	*telephone box*
la guía de	
teléfonos	*directory*
información	*directory enquiries*
la llamada a cobro	
revertido	*reverse charge call*
el número	
de teléfono	*telephone number*
el prefijo	*telephone code*
la tarjeta	
telefónica	*telephone card*
marcar	*dial; tap in*

LAS DIRECCIONES
DIRECTIONS

¿Donde está . . .?

a la derecha	*on the right*	todo recto/	
a la izquierda	*on the left*	seguido	*straight ahead*

¿Cómo puedo llegar a . . . ?	*How do I get to . . . ?*
¿A qué distancia está?	*How far is it?*
¿Está lejos de aquí?	*Is it far from here?*
¿Está cerca de aquí?	*Is it near here?*

¿Se puede ir andando?	*Can I get there on foot?*
Coja la primera (calle) a la derecha/izquierda.	*You take the first road on the right / left.*
Vaya hasta el cruce/el semáforo/el puente.	*Go to the crossing / lights / bridge.*
Cruce la carretera/el puente/ la plaza.	*Cross the road / bridge / square.*
Coja el paso subterráneo.	*Take the underpass.*
Cuando llegue a . . . gire . . .	*When you come to the . . . you turn . . .*
(No) está lejos.	*It's (not) far.*
Está a cien metros/cinco minutos.	*It's 100 metres / 5 minutes away.*
¿Se puede ir en autobús/coche?	*Can I get there by bus / car?*
Coja . . .	*Take . . .*
el autobús número . . .	*the number . . . bus*
el metro	*the underground*
el tren	*the train*
. . . y bájese en la parada . . .	*. . . and get off at the stop . . .*
¿Cada cuánto tiempo hay trenes?	*How often do the trains run?*
Cada (diez minutos)	*Every (ten minutes)*

12 **La ciudad y las compras** *Town and shopping*

¿Cuánto cuesta?	*How much does it cost?*
Puede comprar (un bonobús)	*You can buy a (multi journey bus card.)*
¿Dónde puedo comprar uno?	*Where can I get one?*
En correos/un estanco/un quiosco	*At the post office / tobacconist's / kiosk*
¿Dónde está . . . ?	*Where is . . . ?*
Tiene que cancelar/formalizar su billete.	*You have to cancel / validate your ticket.*

Cuando llegue allí, está . . .	*When you get there it's . . .*
a la izquierda/a la derecha	*on the left / right*
dentro del edificio	*inside the building*
al lado de la fuente	*beside the fountain*
al pie de las escaleras	*at the bottom of the steps*
frente al parque	*opposite the park*
camino del castillo	*on the way to the castle*
frente a la iglesia	*facing the church*

Tiene que ir . . .	*You have to go . . .*
a la izquierda/a la derecha del museo	*to the left / right of the museum*
a lo largo de la orilla del río	*along the river bank*
por el puente	*over the bridge*
pasando el monumento	*past the memorial*

¡Aquí está!	*It's right here!*
Está . . .	*It's . . .*
por allí	*over there*
allí arriba	*up there*
allí abajo	*down there*
en algún sitio	*somewhere*
¡No sé donde está!	*I don't know where it is!*

12 La ciudad y las compras *Town and shopping*

andar	*to walk*	girar	*to turn*
coger	*to take*	pasar	*to pass*
conducir	*to drive*	seguir	*to follow*
cruzar	*to cross*		

13 Los viajes y el turismo *Travel and tourism*

LOS VIAJES
TRAVEL

la excursión	*excursion*
el horario	*timetable*
la llegada	*arrival*
la salida	*departure*
el tour; el recorrido turístico	*tour*
la travesía	*voyage*
el viaje	*journey*

Viajando en tren
Travel by train

el andén	*platform*
el billete	*ticket*
el billete de ida	*single ticket*
el billete de ida y vuelta	*return ticket*
el billete con descuento	*cheap ticket*
la estación (de ferrocarril) - RENFE	*station*
la media tarifa	*half fare*
el/la pasajero-a	*passenger*
el retraso	*delay*
la tarifa completa	*full fare*
la venta automática de billetes	*automatic ticket sales*

Los trenes — Trains

la AVE (Alta Velocidad Española)	*high-speed intercity train*
el expreso/ el TALGO	*express*
el mercancías	*freight train*
el motorail	*motorail*
el rápido	*fast train*
el tren correo	*slow / mail train*
el tren de cercanías	*local train*
el tren de largo recorrido	*Inter-city*
eléctrico	*electric*
diesel	*diesel*
de vapor	*steam*
las agujas	*points*
la cafetería	*buffet car*
el coche-cama	*sleeper*
las líneas eléctricas aéreas	*overhead cables*
la litera	*couchette*
el motor	*engine*
los raíles	*rails*
las señales	*signals*
el vagón; el coche	*railway carriage*
el vagón-restaurante	*restaurant car*
las vías	*lines*

¿Es necesario reservar billete con antelación?	*Do you have to book in advance?*
¿A qué hora sale el tren?	*What time does the train leave?*
¿De qué andén?	*From which platform?*
¿Tengo que hacer transbordo?	*Do I have to change?*
¿Es éste el tren de . . . ?	*Is this the train for . . . ?*

Fumador	*Smoking*
No Fumador	*Non-smoking*
anular un billete	*to cancel a ticket*
cambiar un billete	*to change a ticket*
formalizar un billete	*to validate a ticket*
reservar con antelación	*to book in advance*
reservar un asiento	*to reserve a seat*
viajar sin billete	*to travel without a ticket*

Viajando en avión
Travel by plane

la aduana	*customs*
el aeropuerto	*airport*
la cinta de equipajes	*luggage carousel*
la clase preferente	*first class*
la clase turista	*economy class*
la etiqueta de equipaje	*luggage label*
la facturación	*check-in*
el formulario de inmigración	*immigration form*
la inmigración	*immigration*
las llegadas	*arrivals*
la puerta número . . .	*gate . . .*
la sala de salidas	*departure lounge*
las salidas	*departures*
la tarjeta de embarque	*boarding card*
la tienda libre de impuestos	*duty-free shop*
el viajero	*passenger*

el viajero en tránsito	*transit passenger*
el vuelo	*flight*
el vuelo chárter	*charter flight*
el vuelo regular	*scheduled flight*
diríjanse al mostrador/ puerta . . .	*go to desk / gate . . .*
el accidente de aviación	*plane crash*
el ala	*wing*
el ascensor	*lift*
el asiento	*seat*
el asiento de pasillo	*aisle / corridor seat*
el asiento de ventanilla	*window seat*
el aterrizaje	*landing*
el aterrizaje forzoso	*crash landing*
los auriculares	*head set*
la avería de motor	*engine trouble*
la azafata	*stewardess*
el bache	*air pocket*
la cabina	*cabin*
el chaleco salvavidas	*life jacket*
el cinturón de seguridad	*safety belt*
la cola	*queue*
la cola (de avión)	*tail*
el control de pasaportes	*passport control*
el copiloto	*second pilot*
el despegue	*take off*
el equipaje	*luggage*
la escalera	*stairs*
los escalones	*steps*
la fila	*row*
el fuselaje	*fuselage*
la hélice	*propeller*

el jet; el avión a reacción	*jet*
la mesa	*table*
el navegante	*navigator*
las normas de seguridad	*safety regulations*
el número de asiento	*seat number*
el pasaporte	*passport*
el piloto	*pilot*
la pista	*runway*
la puerta	*door*
la salida	*way out*
la salida de emergencia	*emergency exit*
la tripulación	*crew*
la turbulencia	*turbulence*
aterrizar	*to land*
despegar	*to take off*

Viajando en barco
Travel by boat

el contador (de navío)	*purser*
el crucero	*cruise*
la cubierta	*deck*
el ferry	*ferry*
el oficial de navío	*ship's officer*
la plancha	*gang plank*
las puertas de embarque de vehículos	*vehicle loading doors*
la rampa	*ramp*
la tripulación	*crew*

El mar está . . .	*The sea is . . .*
revuelto	*rough*
tranquilo	*smooth*

navegar	*to sail*
marearse	*to be sea sick*

atracar al muelle	*to dock*

Viajando en autobús
Travel by bus

el asiento	*seat*
el conductor	*driver*
la estación de autobuses	*bus station*
la parada de autobús	*bus stop*
el pasillo	*aisle*
el precio del viaje; el billete	*fare*
el horario de autobuses	*bus timetable*

¿A qué hora sale/llega el autobús?	*What time does the bus leave / arrive?*
¿Cuánto vale el billete?	*How much is the ticket?*
¿De dónde sale el autobús?	*Where does the bus leave from?*
¿Dónde está la parada?	*Where's the bus stop?*

13 Los viajes y el turismo *Travel and tourism*

VIAJANDO EN BICICLETA/EN MOTO
TRAVEL BY BICYCLE/MOTORBIKE

(See also *Hobbies and sports*, page 116.)

la bicicleta	*bicycle*
la moto(cicleta)	*motor bike / scooter*

la bomba de bicicleta	*pump*
la cadena	*chain*
la caja de herramientas	*repair kit*
los frenos	*brakes*
el manillar	*handle bars*
el neumático	*tyre*
el pinchazo	*puncture*
las ruedas	*wheels*
el sillín	*saddle*

¡OTRA VEZ!

● *Activity: how do you prefer to travel?*

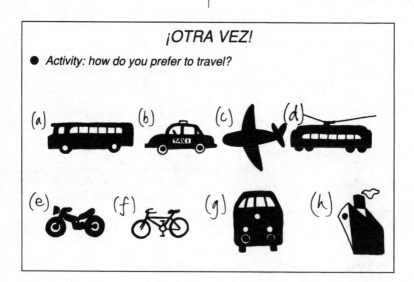

13 Los viajes y el turismo *Travel and tourism*

EL TURISMO
TOURISM

la agencia de viajes	*travel agent*
el agroturismo	*country holidays*
la anulación	*cancellation*
los billetes	*tickets*
el folleto	*brochure*
la hoja de reserva	*booking form*
las inyecciones; las vacunas	*jabs; inoculations*
el seguro	*insurance*
el visado	*visa*

Las zonas de veraneo
Holiday areas

el lugar de veraneo; el centro turístico	*holiday resort*
el parque nacional	*national park*
el parque temático	*theme park*

Zonas Populares en España
Popular Areas in Spain

Las Costas	**Coasts**
La Costa del Sol	*(south east Mediterranean)*
La Costa Brava	*(north east Mediterranean)*
La Costa Verde	*(north coast of Spain)*
Las Islas	**Islands**
Las Islas Baleares	*The Balearics*
Las Islas Canarias	*The Canaries*
Las Montañas	**Mountains**
Los Picos de Europa	*(northern Spain, near Santander)*
Los Pirineos	*(between France and Spain)*
La Sierra Nevada	*(southern Spain, near Granada)*
El Coto Doñana	*Doñana National Park (south west Spain)*

Me gusta pasar mis vacaciones . . .	*I like to spend my holidays . . .*
en el campo	*in the country*
en casa	*at home*
en una ciudad	*in a city*
en el mar	*at sea*
en la montaña	*in the mountains*
en la playa	*at the sea-side*

Prefiero . . .	*I prefer . . .*
unas vacaciones tranquilas	*a quiet holiday*
unas vacaciones en el extranjero	*an overseas holiday*
unas vacaciones en la playa	*a seaside holiday*

unas vacaciones con actividades	*an activity holiday*
un viaje	*a trip*
un tour	*a tour*
un crucero	*a cruise*
viajar de mochila	*back packing*
el senderismo	*a walking holiday*
el descanso de fin de semana	*a weekend holiday*
una excursión	*a day trip*
unas vacaciones llenas de aventuras	*an adventure holiday*
unas vacaciones con mis amigos	*a holiday with my friends*
Quiero ir a sitios de interés turístico.	*I want to see the sights.*

un anfiteatro	*amphitheatre*	un valle	*valley*
un bosque	*forest*	una vista	*view*
una casa			
solariega	*stately home*	El/la turista	*The tourist*
un castillo	*castle*	el/la visitante	*visitor*
una catedral	*cathedral*	el/la viajero-a	*traveller*
unas cuevas	*caves*	el/la que viaja	
un edificio		con mochila	*backpacker*
histórico	*historic building*	el/la veraneante	*holiday maker*
una iglesia	*church*	el/la gamberro-a	
un lago	*lake*	de litrona	*'lager lout'*
el lugar de			
nacimiento	*the birthplace*	el adaptador	
de ...	*of ...*	eléctrico	*electric adaptor*
un mar;		las botas/los	
un océano	*sea*	zapatos para	
una mezquita	*mosque*	caminar	*walking boots / shoes*
un monasterio	*abbey*	la cámara; máquina	
una montaña	*mountain*	de fotos	*camera*
un monumento	*monument*	el cinturón para	
un monumento		el dinero	*money belt*
antiguo	*ancient monument*	la crema para después	
un museo	*museum*	del sol	*after-sun cream*
un puente	*bridge*	la guía	*guide; guide book*
un río	*river*	el libro de frases	*phrase book*
unas ruinas		la maleta	*suitcase*
romanas/	*Roman / Moorish*	el mapa	*map*
árabes	*ruins*	la mochila	*ruck sack*
		el pasaporte	*passport*

13 Los viajes y el turismo *Travel and tourism*

el plano de la ciudad	*town plan*	alojarse	*to stay*
el protector solar	*sun cream / lotion*	comprar	*to buy*
		filmar	*to film*
el repelente de insectos	*insect repellent*	hacer fotos	*to photograph*
		ir al extranjero	*to go abroad*
el recuerdo	*souvenir*	reservar	*to book*
la riñonera	*bum bag*	viajar	*to travel*
		visitar	*to visit*

El alojamiento *Holiday accommodation*

Vamos a alojarnos en . . .	We are going to stay . . .
un albergue para jóvenes	*in a youth hostel*
un apartamento	*in an apartment*
un camping	*on a camp site*
una fonda	*at an inn*
una granja	*on a farm*
un hostal	*in a boarding house*
un hotel	*in an hotel*
un parador	*in a parador (luxury state hotel)*
una pensión	*at a guest house*

la pensión completa	*full board*	la llave	*key*
la media pensión	*half board*	la piscina	*pool*
		el portero	*porter*
en el hotel	*in the hotel*	la recepción	*reception*
el ascensor	*lift*	la reserva	*reservation*
el bar	*bar*	el restaurante	*restaurant*
la cama	*bed*		
las escaleras	*stairs*	el comedor	*dining room*
el gimnasio	*fitness room*	el salón	*lounge*
la habitación	*bedroom*	la tienda	*shop*
		el vestuario	*changing room*

una habitación . . .	a . . . room
doble	double
individual	single

una habitación con . . .	a room with . . .
aire acondicionado	air conditioning
baño	bath
ducha	shower
instalaciones para minusválidos	disabled facilities
teléfono	phone
televisión	TV
terraza	balcony
vistas al mar	sea view

¿Qué precio tiene la habitación?	How much is the room?
¿Está incluido el desayuno?	Is breakfast included?

¿A qué hora se sirve . . .	What time is . . .
el desayuno?	breakfast?
la comida?	lunch?
la cena?	dinner?

Quisiera reservar/cancelar una habitación.	I'd like to reserve/cancel a room.
Tengo una habitación reservada a nombre de . . .	I have a room reserved in the name of . . .

El aire acondicionado no funciona.	The air conditioning isn't working.
Necesito otra toalla.	I need another towel.
No hay jabón.	There's no soap.

En el camping
On the camp-site

el agua	water	las duchas	showers
el aparcamiento	parking	la electricidad	electricity
la autocaravana	camper van	el emplazamiento	site
la basura	refuse	los fregaderos	sinks
la caravana	caravan	el lavadero	washing facilities
		los servicios	toilets
		la tienda	tent

En el albergue para jóvenes
In the youth hostel

la cocina	*kitchen*
el comedor	*dining room*
el dormitorio	*dormitory*
las normas	*regulations*

el salón	
de recreo	*recreation room*
los servicios	*toilets*
el/la vigilante	*warden*

Rellene la ficha, por favor.   *Fill in the form, please*

Nombre	*Name*
Dirección	*Address*
Lugar de	
Nacimiento	*Place of birth*
Fecha de	
Nacimiento	*Date of birth*
Nacionalidad	*Nationality*
Matrícula de	
Coche	*Car registration*
Fecha de	
Llegada	*Date of arrival*
Fecha de Salida	*Date of departure*
Número de Carnet	
de Identidad/	
Pasaporte	*Identity card /*
	passport number

En el mar *At sea*

el acantilado	*cliffs*
la boya	*buoy*
el faro	*lighthouse*
la isla	*island*
el mar	*sea*
el muelle	*dock*
el puerto	*port*
las rocas	*rocks*

la barca	*boat*
el barco	*ship*
el barco de	
pesca	*fishing boat*

el barco de vapor	*steamship*
el barco	
rastreador	*trawler*
el buque	
contenedor	*container ship*
el ferry	*ferry*
la lancha	
motora	*motor boat*
el submarino	*submarine*
el transatlántico	*cruise liner*
el velero	*sailing ship*

el ancla	*anchor*
la cabina	*cabin*
la chimenea	*funnel*
el motor	*engine*
la popa	*stern*
la proa	*bows*
el puente	*bridge*
el radar	*radar*
el timón	*rudder*
las velas	*sails*

babor y estribor	*port and starboard*
el capitán	*captain*
el marinero	*sailor*
la niebla	*fog*
la sirena	
de niebla	*fog horn*
la tempestad	*gale*
la tripulación	*crew*

13 Los viajes y el turismo *Travel and tourism*

achicar	*to bail out*
echar vapor	*to steam*
gobernar	*to steer*
navegar	*to sail*
el bote salvavidas	*lifeboat*
el cinturón salvavidas	*lifebelt*
el embarque	*embarcation*
el iceberg	*iceberg*
el naufragio	*shipwreck*
ahogarse	*to drown*
chocar con una roca	*to hit a rock*
hundirse	*to sink*
nadar	*to swim*
naufragar	*to be shipwrecked*
rescatar	*to rescue*

En la playa *At the sea-side*

(See also *Hobbies and Sports*, page 117.)

las aletas	*flippers*
el alga	*seaweed*
la arena	*sand*
el bañador	*swimming costume*
la crema bronceadora	*sun cream*
la crema para después del sol	*after-sun cream*
el cubo y la pala	*bucket and spade*
la duna	*dune*
las gafas de sol	*sunglasses*
los guijarros	*shingle*
la loción para las quemaduras de sol	*sunburn lotion*
el mar	*sea*
la marea	*tide*
la marea alta	*high tide*
la marea baja	*low tide*
el pic-nic; la merienda	*picnic*
la playa	*beach*
la protección contra el viento	*wind break*
el protector solar	*sunblock*
el puesto de los helados	*ice-cream kiosk*
la sombrilla	*parasol*
la toalla	*towel*
el tubo de respiración	*snorkel*
la tumbona	*deck chair*
bañarse	*to swim*
hacer castillos de arena	*to build sandcastles*
relajarse; descansar	*to relax*
tomar el sol	*to sunbathe*

13 Los viajes y el turismo *Travel and tourism*

LOS COCHES Y EL AUTOMOVILISMO
CARS AND MOTORING

el accidente	*accident*
las carreteras	*roads*
las señales de tráfico /de carreteras	*road signs*

En el taller *At the garage*

Las piezas del coche y los accesorios — **Car parts and accessories**

los accesorios	*accessories*
el airbag	*airbag*
la aleta	*wing*
los asientos	*seats*
la baca	*roof / roof rack*
la batería	*battery*
las bombillas de repuesto	*spare bulbs*
el botiquín	*first aid kit*
las bujías	*spark plugs*
la caja de cambios	*gear box*
el capó	*bonnet*
la carrocería	*body*
el catalizador	*catalytic converter*
la cerradura	*lock*
el chasis	*chassis*
el claxon	*horn*
el coche	*car*
la correa del ventilador	*fanbelt*
el depósito de la gasolina	*petrol tank*
la dirección asistida	*power assisted steering*
el embrague	*clutch*
los faros	*head lamps*
los frenos	*brakes*
los frenos ABS	*ABS brakes*
el gato	*jack*
los guantes de plástico	*plastic gloves*
los intermitentes	*indicators*
el lavaparabrisas	*screen wash*
los limpiaparabrisas	*windscreen wipers*
las luces cortas	*dipped headlights*
las luces largas	*full beam*
las luces de posición	*side lights*
las llaves	*keys*
el maletero	*boot*
el motor	*engine*
el neumático	*tyre*
el parachoques	*bumper*
las piezas	*parts*
la puerta	*door*
el retrovisor	*wing mirror*
la rueda	*wheel*
el tapón de la gasolina	*petrol cap*
el triángulo señalizador	*warning triangle*
el tubo de escape	*exhaust pipe*
la velocidad/ la marcha	*gear*
la ventanilla	*window*
el volante	*steering wheel*
el coche automático	*automatic car*
el coche con puerta trasera	*hatch back*
el coche deportivo	*sports car*
fórmula uno	*formula 1*

13 Los viajes y el turismo *Travel and tourism*

Las prestaciones	**Performance**
el consumo	*fuel consumption*
la dirección	*steering*
los frenos	*braking*
la potencia (en caballos)	*horse power*
la velocidad	*speed*
el tren/el túnel de lavado de coches	*car wash*
la cera de coche	*car wax*
el/la aprendiz-a de conductor-a	*learner driver*
la autoescuela	*driving school*
el carnet de conducir	*driving licence*
el carnet de conducir provisional	*provisional licence*
el impuesto de circulación	*road tax*
la ITV	*MOT*
el manual	*manual*
el seguro . . .	*. . . insurance*
a terceros	*third party*
a todo riesgo	*comprehensive*
el accidente	*accident*
la asistencia	*assistance*
el atasco; el embotellamiento	*traffic jam; hold up*
el auxilio en carretera	*breakdown assistance*
la avería	*breakdown*
el choque en cadena	*pile up*
la colisión; el choque	*collision*

el pinchazo	*puncture*
el RACE	*AA / RAC (equivalent)*
la reparación	*repair*
el teléfono de emergencia	*emergency telephone*

Las carreteras y señales de tráfico
Roads and road signs

la autopista	*motorway*
la autovía	*dual carriageway*
la carretera nacional	*main road*
la calle de dirección única	*one-way street*
el callejón sin salida	*cul de sac*
la carretera comarcal	*country road*
el arcén	*hard shoulder*
el bordillo	*verge*
el carril	*lane*
el carril de adelantamiento	*overtaking lane*
la curva	*bend*
el desvío	*diversion*
el límite de velocidad	*speed restriction*
las obras de carretera	*road works*
el peaje	*toll*
el semáforo	*traffic lights*
las señales de emergencia	*emergency lights*
prohibido adelantar	*no overtaking*

13 Los viajes y el turismo *Travel and tourism*

En la estación de servico
At the services

el aceite	*oil*
el anti-congelante	*anti-freeze*
la bombilla	*light bulb*
la gasolina . . .	*. . . petrol*
con plomo	*leaded*
sin plomo	*unleaded*
súper	*four star*
el gas-oil	*diesel*
la gasolinera	*petrol station*
el líquido de frenos	*brake fluid*
el mapa de carreteras	*road map*
la presión de los neumáticos	*tyre pressure*
el surtidor de gasolina	*petrol pump*
la carta verde	*green card*

la documentación del coche	*car papers*
el seguro	*insurance*
adelantar	*to overtake*
atropellar	*to run over*
cambiar de velocidad	*to change gear*
chocar con	*to collide*
conducir	*to drive*
dar contra	*to hit*
dar marcha atrás	*to reverse*
derrapar	*to skid*
dirigir; manejar	*to steer*
exceder la velocidad permitida	*to speed*
frenar	*to brake*
perder el control	*to lose control*
quedarse sin gasolina	*to run out of petrol*
recalentar	*to overheat*
tener una avería	*to break down*
torcer (bruscamente)	*to swerve*

Expressiones útiles *Useful expressions*

¡Lleno, por favor!	*Fill her up!*
Mi coche no arranca	*My car won't start*
¿Puede comprobar . . .	*Could you check . . .*
el aceite	*the oil*
el agua	*the water*
la presión	*the tyre pressures?*
Me he quedado sin gasolina	*I've run out of petrol*
El motor se calienta mucho	*The engine's overheating*
¿Hay un taller de reparaciones cerca, por favor?	*Is there a garage near here, please?*
¿Arreglan pinchazos?	*Do you repair punctures?*
Quisiera alquilar un coche	*I'd like to hire a car*
¿Puedo pagar con tarjeta de crédito?	*Can I pay by credit card?*

14 **La naturaleza** *The natural world*

EL CAMPO
THE COUNTRYSIDE

El paisaje *Landscape*

el campo	*country*
el pueblo	*village*
la iglesia	*church*
el arroyo	*stream*
la cascada	*waterfall*
el desierto	*desert*
el estanque	*pond*
el lago	*lake*
la llanura	*plain*
la marisma	*marsh*
el río	*river*
las rocas	*rocks*
el valle	*valley*
la colina	*hill*
la cumbre	*summit*
el funicular	*funicular*
la montaña	*mountain*
el pico	*mountain peak*
la sierra	*mountain range*
el teleférico	*cable railway*
el camino	*path*
la pradera	*grassland*
el prado	*field*
la puerta	*gate*
el sendero	*footpath*
el seto	*hedge*
la tapia	*wall*

Los árboles *Trees*

el bosque	*wood*
la selva	*forest*

Los árboles de hoja caduca	**Deciduous trees**
el abedul	*silver birch*
el álamo	*poplar*
el alcornoque	*cork tree*
el arce	*maple*
el castaño	*chestnut*
el eucalipto	*eucalyptus*
el fresno	*ash*
la haya	*beech*
la magnolia	*magnolia*
el roble	*oak*
el sauce	*willow*
el sicomoro	*sycamore*

Los árboles coníferos	**Coniferous trees**
el abeto	*fir*
el alerce	*larch*
el pino	*pine*

Los frutales	**Fruit trees**
el aguacate	*avocado*
el albaricoquero	*apricot*
el almendro	*almond*
el ciruelo	*plum*
la higuera	*fig*
el limonero	*lemon*
el manzano	*apple*
el melocotonero	*peach*
el naranjo	*orange*
el olivo	*olive*
la palmera	*palm*
el peral	*pear*

andar; caminar	*to walk*
dar una caminata	*to hike*
dar una carrera; correr	*to go for a run*
montar en bicicleta	*to cycle*
montar a caballo	*to ride*
merendar en el campo	*to have a picnic*

14 La naturaleza *The natural world*

¡OTRA VEZ!

● *Activity:* ¿Qué significan estos símbolos? *What do the symbols mean?*

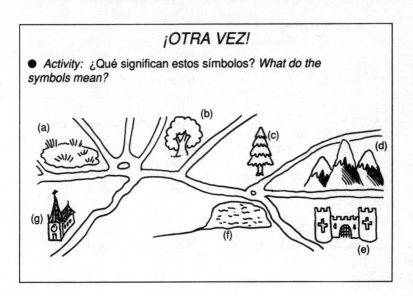

14 **La naturaleza** *The natural world*

EN LA GRANJA
ON THE FARM

la granja	*farm*
los edificios de la granja	*farm buildings*
el corral	*farm yard*
la tierra de labranza	*farm land*
la casa de campo	*farmhouse*
la agricultura	*arable farming*
el cobertizo; la nave	*shed*
la cuadra	*stable*
el establo	*stall*
la ganadería	*cattle*
los lácteos	*dairy*
el ganado vacuno	*beef*
el granero	*barn*

Los animales domésticos
Farm animals

el/la ternero-a	*calf*
el toro	*bull*
la vaca	*cow*
el asno	*donkey*
el caballo	*horse*
el caballo de tiro	*cart horse*
el/la mulo-a	*mule*
el poney	*pony*
el potro	*foal*
el semental	*stallion*
la yegua	*mare*
el carnero	*ram*
el cordero	*lamb*
la oveja	*sheep*
la cerda	*sow*

el cerdo	*pig*
el cochinillo	*piglet*
el verraco	*boar*
la cabra	*goat*
el cabrito; el chivo	*kid*

Las aves de corral *Poultry*

la gallina	*hen*
el gallo	*cockerel*
el pollo	*chicken*
el ansarino	*gosling*
el ganso	*gander*
la oca	*goose*
el patito	*duckling*
el pato	*duck*
el arado	*plough*
la cosechadora	*combine harvester*
el tractor	*tractor*
la avena	*oats*
la cebada	*barley*
el centeno	*rye*
el grano	*grain*
el heno	*hay*
el maíz	*corn*
la paja	*straw*
el trigo	*wheat*
la cerca	*fence*
el corral	*paddock*
cosechar	*to harvest*
cultivar	*to cultivate*
dar de comer a los animales	*to feed the animals*
plantar	*plant*
regar	*to irrigate*
sembrar	*to sow*

LOS ANIMALES
ANIMALS

la ardilla	*squirrel*
la comadreja	*weasel*
el conejo	*rabbit*
el gusano	*worm*
el hurón	*ferret*
la liebre	*hare*
el lobo	*wolf*
la mofeta	*skunk*

LA CAZA MAYOR Y OTROS MAMÍFEROS
BIG GAME AND OTHER MAMMALS

el antílope	*antelope*
la ballena	*whale*
el bisonte	*bison*
el búfalo	*buffalo*
el camello	*camel*
la cebra	*zebra*
el canguro	*kangaroo*
el chimpancé	*chimpanzee*
el ciervo	*reindeer*
el coala	*koala*
el delfín	*dolphin*
el elefante	*elephant*
la foca	*seal*
el gorila	*gorilla*
el hipopótamo	*hippopotamus*
la hiena	*hyena*
el jaguar	*jaguar*
el jabalí	*wild boar*
la jirafa	*giraffe*
el león	*lion*
el leopardo	*leopard*
el mono	*monkey*
el oso	*brown bear*

la nutria	*otter*
el puerco espín	*hedgehog*
la rana	*frog*
la rata	*rat*
el sapo	*toad*
el tejón	*badger*
el topo	*mole*
el visón	*mink*
el zorro	*fox*

la pantera	*panther*
el rinoceronte	*rhinoceros*
la serpiente	*snake*
el tigre	*tiger*

Las partes del cuerpo de un animal
Parts of the animal

las astas	*horns; antlers*
los bigotes	*whiskers*
el caparazón; la concha	*shell*
la cola	*tail*
el colmillo	*tusk*
la cornamenta	*antlers*
el cuerno	*horn*
la escama	*scale*
la giba	*hump*
el hocico	*snout*
la pata	*paw*
el pelo	*coat*
la pezuña	*hoof*
el pellejo	*skin*
la piel	*fur*
la púa	*spike*
la trompa	*trunk*
la zarpa	*claw*

LOS PÁJAROS; LAS AVES
BIRDS

el águila	*eagle*
el águila pescadora	*osprey*
el águila real	*golden eagle*
la agachadiza	*snipe*
la alondra	*skylark*
el avión	*martin*
el búho	*owl*
el buitre	*vulture*
la cigüeña	*stork*
el cisne	*swan*
el cormorán	*cormorant*
el cuco; el cuclillo	*cuckoo*
el cuervo	*crow*
el estornino	*starling*
el faisán	*pheasant*
el gavilán	*hawk*
la gaviota	*seagull*
la golondrina	*swallow*
el gorrión	*sparrow*
el grajo	*rook*
el halcón	*falcon*

el herrerillo	*blue-tit*
la lechuza	*barn owl*
el martín pescador	*kingfisher*
el mirlo	*blackbird*
la paloma	*dove*
el palomo; el pichón	*pigeon*
el pelícano	*pelican*
la perdiz	*partridge*
el petirrojo	*robin*
el pinzón	*chaffinch*
el ruiseñor	*nightingale*
la urraca	*magpie*
el vencejo	*swift*
el zorzal	*thrush*

el ala	*wing*
el huevo	*egg*
el nido	*nest*
el pico	*beak*
la pluma	*feather*
la zarpa; la uña	*claw*

la ornitología	*ornithology*
observar aves	*bird-watching*

INSECTOS
INSECTS

la abeja	*bee*
la colmena	*bee-hive*
el panal	*honey comb*
la miel	*honey*
la araña	*spider*
la tela de araña	*spider's web*
la avispa	*wasp*
el nido de avispa	*wasp's nest*

la cucaracha	*cockroach*
el grillo	*cricket*
el gusano	*grub; maggot*
la hormiga	*ant*
la libélula	*dragonfly*
la mariposa	*butterfly / moth*
la mariquita	*ladybird*
la mosca	*fly*
el mosquito	*mosquito*
la oruga	*caterpillar*
la pulga	*flea*
el saltamontes	*grasshopper*
el tábano	*horse fly*
la típula	*cranefly*

14 La naturaleza *The natural world*

cazar	*to hunt*	ladrar	*to bark*
la caza	*hunting*	maullar	*to miaow*
disparar	*to shoot*	mugir	*to moo*
		relinchar	*to neigh*
aullar	*to howl*	ronronear	*to purr*
balar	*to bleat*	rugir	*to roar*
cacarear	*to crow*	silbar	*to hiss*
gatear	*to crawl*	ulular	*to hoot*
gruñir	*to grunt*	zumbar	*to buzz*

Temas del medio ambiente
Environmental issues

el medio ambiente	*environment*
la contaminación	*environmental pollution*
el agujero en la capa de ozono	*hole in the ozone layer*
el alga tóxica	*toxic alga*
la biosfera	*biosphere*
el calentamiento global	*global warming*
la capa de ozono	*ozone layer*
los CFCs	*CFC's*
la contaminación del agua	*water pollution*
la contaminación del aire	*air pollution*
la contaminación urbana	*urban pollution*
la deforestación de la selva tropical	*destruction of the rain forest*
la desertización	*desertisation*
la destrucción del habitat	*destruction of the habitat*
la destrucción del medio ambiente	*destruction of the environment*
la ecología	*ecology*
los ecologistas	*ecologists*
el efecto invernadero	*greenhouse effect*
la erosión del suelo	*soil erosion*

14 La naturaleza *The natural world*

los fertilizantes	*fertilizers*	el carbón	*coal*
la lluvia ácida	*acid rain*	la central	
la marea negra	*oil slick*	eléctrica	*power station*
la niebla tóxica	*smog*	la central	*nuclear power*
el Partido Verde	*Green Party*	nuclear	*station*
los pesticidas	*pesticides*	el combustible	*fuel*
la política verde	*green politics*	el combustible	
la protección		nuclear	*nuclear fuel*
medio-	*environmental*	el combustible	
ambiental	*protection*	sólido	*solid fuel*
los rayos		la energía	
ultravioletas	*ultraviolet rays*	nuclear	*nuclear power*
el reciclaje	*re-cycling*	la fusión	
los recursos		nuclear	*nuclear fusion*
naturales	*natural resources*	el gas	*gas*
el rescate		el petróleo	*oil*
de terrenos	*land reclamation*	la radiación	*radiation*
los residuos		los vertidos	
radioactivos	*radioactive waste*	nucleares	*nuclear waste*
la selva tropical	*rain forest*		
la super-			
población	*overpopulation*		

la energía ...	*... power / energy*
eólica	*wind*
hidroeléctrica	*hydroelectric*
de las mareas	*tidal*
solar	*solar*
las energías renovables	*renewable energy*
la protección de los animales	*protection of animals*
la protección del medio ambiente	*protection of the environment*

ahorrar	*to save*	destruir	*to destroy*
conservar	*to conserve*	malgastar	*to waste*
contaminar	*to contaminate;*	proteger	*to protect*
	pollute	reciclar	*to recycle*

14 La naturaleza *The natural world*

EL TIEMPO Y EL CLIMA
WEATHER AND THE CLIMATE

El tiempo *The weather*

el aire	*air*
la atmósfera	*atmosphere*
el barómetro	*barometer*
el calor	*heat*
el cielo	*sky*
el clima	*climate*
el frío	*cold*
la humedad	*humidity*
la precipitación	*rainfall*
el pronóstico (del tiempo)	*forecast*
la sequía	*drought*
el termómetro	*thermometer*
la visibilidad	*visibility*
el aguacero; el chaparrón	*downpour*
el aguanieve	*sleet*
el arco iris	*rainbow*
la brisa	*breeze*
el chubasco	*shower*
los claros	*bright intervals*
el granizo	*hail*
la helada	*frost*
el hielo	*ice*
la inundación	*flood*
la llovizna	*drizzle*
la lluvia	*rain*
el mal tiempo	*bad weather*
la neblina	*mist*
la niebla	*fog*
la nieve	*snow*
la bola de nieve	*snowball*
el muñeco de nieve	*snowman*
el quitanieves	*snowplough*
la nevada	*snowstorm*
la nube	*cloud*
la ola de calor/frío	*heat wave / cold snap*
la racha de viento	*gust*
el rocío	*dew*
el sol	*sun*
el torbellino	*whirlwind*
la tormenta	*storm*
el trueno y el relámpago	*thunder and lightning*
el viento	*wind*
de Levante	*East wind*
de Poniente	*West wind*
las altas presiones	*high pressure*
las bajas presiones	*low pressure*
la borrasca	*storm*
el frente cálido	*warm front*
la gota fría	*cold front*

Hace . . .	It is . . .
calor	*hot*
fresco	*cool*
frío	*cold*
humedad	*humid*
niebla	*foggy; misty*
viento	*windy*
buen tiempo	*fine*

173

14 **La naturaleza** *The natural world*

un tiempo lluvioso	*rainy*
un tiempo pesado	*heavy*
un tiempo seco	*dry*
un tiempo templado	*mild*
un tiempo variable	*changeable*
Está/estaba . . .	*It is / it was . . .*
granizando	*hailing*
helando	*freezing*
lloviendo	*raining*
nevando	*snowing*
nublado	*cloudy*
El cielo está . . .	*The sky is . . .*
azul	*blue*
cubierto	*overcast*
despejado	*clear*
nublado	*cloudy*
oscuro	*dark*

aclarar	*to clear up*	llover	*to rain*
cambiar	*to change*	mejorar	*to improve*
derretir	*to melt*	nevar	*to snow*
deshelar	*to thaw*		
granizar	*to hail*	Habrá . . .	*There will be . . .*
hacer calor	*to be hot*	chubascos	*showers*
hacer frío	*to be cold*	claros	*bright intervals*
hacer sol	*to be sunny*	fuertes vientos	*strong winds*
helar	*to freeze*	nieve	*snow*

15 **El ancho mundo** *The wide world*

EL MUNDO
THE WORLD

el Círculo Polar Antártico	*Antarctic Circle*
el Círculo Polar Ártico	*Arctic Circle*
el ecuador	*equator*
el globo	*the Globe*
la latitud	*latitude*
la longitud	*longitude*
la Tierra	*the Earth*
los trópicos	*the tropics*
el trópico de Capricornio	*Tropic of Capricorn*
el trópico de Cáncer	*Tropic of Cancer*

La brújula *The compass*

Norte	*North*
Sur	*South*
Este	*East*
Oeste	*West*

Los continentes
The continents

África	*Africa*
América	*America*
América del Norte	*North America*
Centroamérica	*Central America*
América del Sur	*South America*
Antártida	*Antarctica*
Asia	*Asia*
Europa	*Europe*
Oceanía	*Oceania*

Otros territorios
Other land masses

el Extremo/Lejano Oriente	*Far East*
la India	*India*
el Oriente Medio	*Middle East*

Los océanos *Oceans*

el Antártico	*Antarctic*
el Ártico	*Arctic*
el Atlántico	*Atlantic*
el Pacífico	*Pacific*
el Índico	*Indian*

Los mares *Seas*

el mar Adriático	*the Adriatic Sea*
Báltico	*Baltic Sea*
del Norte	*North Sea*
Mediterráneo	*Mediterranean*
Negro	*Black Sea*

el canal de la Mancha
the English Channel
el estrecho (de Gibraltar)
the Straits of Gibraltar

15 El ancho mundo *The wide world*

Los Países de Europa y la Unión Europea
The Countries of Europe and the European Union

país	country	adjetivo	adjective
Reino Unido	*United Kingdom*		
Gran Bretaña	*Great Britain*	británico-a	*British*
Inglaterra	*England*	inglés-esa	*English*
Gales	*Wales*	galés-esa	*Welsh*
Irlanda del Norte	*Northern Ireland*	irlandés-esa del Norte	*Northern Irish*
Irlanda	*Ireland*	irlandés-esa del Sur	*Irish*
Escocia	*Scotland*	escocés-esa	*Scottish*
Escandinavia	*Scandinavia*	escandinavo-a	*Scandinavian*
Dinamarca	*Denmark*	danés-esa	*Danish*
Finlandia	*Finland*	finlandés-esa	*Finnish*
Suecia	*Sweden*	sueco-a	*Swedish*
Noruega	*Norway*	noruego-a	*Norwegian*

Europa del Oeste *Western Europe*

Bélgica	*Belgium*	belga	*Belgian*
Francia	*France*	francés-esa	*French*
Alemania	*Germany*	alemán-ana	*German*
Holanda	*Holland*	holandés-esa	*Dutch*
Hungría	*Hungary*	húngaro-a	*Hungarian*
Italia	*Italy*	italiano-a	*Italian*
Luxemburgo	*Luxembourg*	luxemburgués-esa	*Luxembourgish*
Portugal	*Portugal*	portugués-esa	*Portuguese*
España	*Spain*	español-a	*Spanish*
Suiza	*Switzerland*	suizo-a	*Swiss*

Europa Central *Central Europe*

Austria	*Austria*	austríaco-a	*Austrian*
Bosnia	*Bosnia*	bosnio-a	*Bosnian*
Bulgaria	*Bulgaria*	búlgaro-a	*Bulgarian*
Croacia	*Croatia*	croata	*Croat*
Polonia	*Poland*	polaco-a	*Polish*
Eslovaquia	*Slovakia*	eslovaco-a	*Slovak*
Eslovenia	*Slovenia*	esloveno-a	*Slovene*

15 El ancho mundo *The wide world*

Grecia	*Greece*	griego-a	*Greek*
Rumania	*Romania*	rumano-a	*Rumanian*
Rusia	*Russia*	ruso-a	*Russian*
la República Checoslovaca	*Czech Republic*	checo-a	*Czech*
Turquía	*Turkey*	turco-a	*Turkish*

América Latina	***Latin America***		
Argentina	*Argentina*	argentino-a	*Argentinian*
Bolivia	*Bolivia*	boliviano-a	*Bolivian*
Brasil	*Brazil*	brasileño-a	*Brazilian*
Chile	*Chile*	chileno-a	*Chilean*
Colombia	*Colombia*	colombiano-a	*Colombian*
Costa Rica	*Costa Rica*	costarricense	*Costa Rican*
Cuba	*Cuba*	cubano-a	*Cuban*
Ecuador	*Ecuador*	ecuatoriano-a	*Ecuadorian*
El Salvador	*El Salvador*	salvadoreño-a	*Salvadorian*
Guatemala	*Guatemala*	guatemalteco-a	*Guatemalan*
Haití	*Haiti*	haitiano-a	*Haitian*
Honduras	*Honduras*	hondureño-a	*Honduran*
México	*Mexico*	mejicano-a	*Mexican*
Nicaragua	*Nicaragua*	nicaragüense	*Nicaraguan*
Panamá	*Panama*	panameño-a	*Panamanian*
Paraguay	*Paraguay*	paraguayo-a	*Paraguayan*
Perú	*Peru*	peruano-a	*Peruvian*
República Dominicana	*Dominican Republic*	dominicano-a	*Dominican*
Uruguay	*Uruguay*	uruguayo-a	*Uruguayan*
Venezuela	*Venezuela*	venezolano-a	*Venezuelan*

Nationalities

Formed by adjective (without article)

Soy inglés.	*I am English / an Englishman.*
Es española.	*She is Spanish / a Spaniard.*
Los ingleses	*The English*

15 El ancho mundo *The wide world*

¡OTRA VEZ!

● *Activity: How many of the EU countries can you name in Spanish?*

15 El ancho mundo *The wide world*

ORGANISMOS NACIONALES E INTERNACIONALES
NATIONAL AND INTERNATIONAL AGENCIES

Organismos nacionales
National organisations

CEPYME	*small business confederation*
Iberia	*state airline*
INI	*national institute for industry*
ONCE	*national blind association*
RACE	*Spanish RAC*
RENFE	*state railways*
RNE	*state radio*
TVE	*state television*

La Unión Europea
The European Union

el Presidente	*The President*
el Consejo de Europa	*Council of Europe*

Organismos internacionales
World organisations

las Naciones Unidas	*United Nations*
la Organización Mundial de la Salud (OMS)	*World Health Organisation*
la Cruz Roja	*Red Cross*
la OTAN	*NATO*
Greenpeace	*Greenpeace*
el FMI	*International Monetary Fund*

NOTICIAS INTERNACIONALES
INTERNATIONAL NEWS ITEMS

el corresponsal	*correspondant*
las noticias	*news*
el accidente	*accident*
el accidente de aviación	*plane crash*
el alud; la avalancha	*avalanche*
el ciclón	*cyclone*
la colisión de trenes	*train crash*
el corrimiento; el desprendimiento de tierras	*landslide*
el desastre	*disaster*
la epidemia	*epidemic*
la erupción de volcán	*volcano eruption*
la explosión de bomba	*bomb explosion*
el golpe de estado	*coup*
la guerra	*war*
la guerra civil	*civil war*
el hambre	*famine*
el hundimiento	*collapse*
el huracán	*hurricane*
el incendio	*fire*
la inundación	*flood*
la invasión	*invasion*
la ola de calor	*heatwave*
la peste	*plague*
la sequía	*drought*
el terremoto	*earthquake*
el terrorismo	*terrorism*
el tifón	*typhoon*
el tornado	*tornado*

conmocionado/a	*shocked*
herido/a	*wounded*
quemado/a	*burned*
el rehén	*hostage*
el/la superviviente	*survivor*
la víctima	*victim*
escribir; redactar	*to write*
imprimir	*to print*
morir; fallecer	*to die*
ser asesinado-a	*to be assassinated / murdered*
ser herido-a; sufrir heridas	*to be injured*
ser matado-a/ muerto-a (por)	*to be killed (by)*

Titulares de noticias internacionales
International news headlines

31 intoxicados por humo en el metro de Londres

■ **Manifestación de la oposición en México**

■ **Nace un nuevo grupo guerrillero en Colombia**

Accidente en un crucero británico

EL ESPACIO
SPACE

el agujero negro	*black hole*
el año luz	*light year*
el asteroide	*asteroid*
el/la astronauta	*astronaut*
el cometa	*comet*
la constelación	*constellation*
el/la cosmon-	
auta	*cosmonaut*
el cosmos	*cosmos*
el eclipse	*eclipse*
la estación	
espacial	*space station*
la estrella	*star*
el extraterrestre	*alien*
la galaxia	*galaxy*
la luna	*moon*
el meteoro	*meteor; meterorite*
la nave espacial	*spacecraft;*
	spaceship
la nebulosa	*nebula*
el OVNI	*UFO*

el planeta	*planet*
el satélite	*satellite*
el telescopio	*telescope*
el transbordador	
espacial	*shuttle*
el universo	*universe*
la velocidad de	
la luz/del	
sonido	*speed of light / sound*
la Vía Láctea	*Milky Way*
orbitar	*to circle; orbit*

Los planetas *The planets*

Júpiter	*Jupiter*
Marte	*Mars*
Mercurio	*Mercury*
Neptuno	*Neptune*
Plutón	*Pluto*
Saturno	*Saturn*
la Tierra	*Earth*
Urano	*Uranus*
Venus	*Venus*

Los daños son de 20.000 millones de dólares

El huracán «Andrés» va perdiendo violencia al adentrarse en Louisiana

Balance de 17 muertos a su paso por EEUU

16 *Extras*

ABREVIATURAS
ABBREVIATIONS

Sr.	*Mr*
Sra.	*Mrs*
Srta.	*Miss*
D.	*Don*
Dña.	*Doña.*
Dr.	*Doctor (male)*
Dra.	*Doctor (female)*
Dtor.	*Director (male)*
Dtora.	*Director (female)*
Ldo.	*for a graduate (male)*

Lda.	*graduate (female)*
ej.	*e.g.*
C/	*calle*
Av.	*Avenida*
dcha.	*right*
izqda.	*left*
Rte.	*sender (on back of envelope)*
EE.UU	*Estados Unidos*
pta., ptas.	*peseta(s)*
IVA	*VAT*

The first letter or two letters of Spanish car registration numbers correspond to the province in which the care were registered. These are:

AB	Albacete	LU	Lugo
AL	Almería	M	Madrid
AV	Avila	MA	Málaga
B	Barcelona	ML	Melilla
BA	Badajoz	MU	Murcia
BI	Bilbao	NA	Navarra
BU	Burgos	O	Oviedo
CA	Cádiz	OR	Orense
CC	Cácares	P	Palencia
CE	Ceuta	PM	Palma de Mallorca
CO	Córdoba	PO	Pontevedra
CR	Ciudad Real	S	Santander
CS	Castellón	SA	Salamanca
CU	Cuenca	SE	Sevilla
GC	Gran Canaria	SG	Segovia
GE	Gerona	SS	San Sebastián
GR	Granada	T	Tarragona
GU	Guadalajara	TF	Tenerife
H	Huelva	TO	Toledo
HU	Huesca	V	Valencia
J	Jaén	VA	Valladolid
LE	León	Z	Zaragoza
LO	Logroño	ZA	Zamora

16 *Extras*

Expressions of anger/frustration/surprise

¡Joder!
¡Coño!
¡Mierda!

Insulting people

¡Cabrón!
¡Maricón!
¡Gilipollas!
¡Vete a la mierda!
¡Hijo de puta!

Expressions of enthusiasm/disgust

¡Es de puta madre!   *(enthusiasm)*
¡Qué asco!   *(disgust)*

PERDONE, POR FAVOR
EXCUSE ME, PLEASE

¡Socorro!; ¡Auxilio!	*Help!*
¿Habla inglés?	*Do you speak English?*
¡Disculpe! ¡Perdone!	*Sorry! Pardon!*
Lo siento.	*I'm sorry.*
¿Cómo?	*Pardon?*
No comprendo.	*I don't understand.*
¿Puede repetirlo, por favor?	*Can you repeat that please*
Más despacio, por favor	*Can you say it more slowly?*
¿Qué quiere decir eso en inglés?	*What does that mean in English?*
¿Habla . . . ?	*Do you speak . . . ?*
¿Cómo se escribe . . . ?	*How do you spell . . . ?*
¿Puede escribirme eso, por favor?	*Can you write that down for me please?*
¿Puede ayudarme?	*Can you help me?*
¿Comprende?	*Do you understand?*
Por favor.	*Please.*
Gracias.	*Thank you.*
De nada.	*Don't mention it.*
¡Oiga!	*Listen!*

16 *Extras*

Lo siento, no he querido molestarle	*I'm sorry, I did not mean to give offence.*
Lo siento, he entendido mal.	*Sorry, I misunderstood.*
Me temo que no me ha entendido bien.	*I'm afraid you have misunderstood me.*

Ha sido culpa mía.	*It was my fault.*	Aviso	*Warning*
		Peligro	*Danger*
NO ha sido culpa mía	*It was NOT my fault.*	¡Ojo!	*Watch out!*
		¡Cuidado!	*Be careful!*
Ha sido culpa suya.	*It was your fault.*	Peligroso	*Dangerous*

SERVICIOS DE EMERGENCIAS
EMERGENCY SERVICES

la Guardia Civil	*Civil Guard*	los Bomberos	*Fire Brigade*
la Policía Local	*Local Police*	Cruz Roja	*Red Cross*
Protección Civil	*Civil Defence*	Urgencias S.S.	*Ambulance*

Key to the Activities

p. 17 *Morning*: Hola, buenos días!; *Day*: Buenos días!; *Evening*: Buenas tardes!;
Night: Adiós, buenas noches!

p. 18 (a) Buenos días, Sr. Suárez (b) Hola, Conchita (c) Buenos días, Dña. María

p. 19 (a) **93 217 62 92** (Barcelona) = noventa y tres – dos diecisiete – sesenta y dos –
noventa y dos (b) **91 732 80 44** (Madrid) = noventa y uno – siete treinta y dos – ochenta
– cuarenta y cuatro (c) **977 31 28 04** (Tarragona) = nueve setenta y siete – treinta y uno
– veintiocho – cero cuatro (d) **952 73 11 59** (Málaga) = nueve cincuenta y dos – setenta
y tres – once – cincuenta y nueve (e) **945 15 99 01** (Vitoria) = nueve cuarenta y cinco –
quince – noventa y nueve – cero uno

p. 20 1.975 – mil novecientos setenta y cinco; 1.998 – mil novecientos noventa y ocho;
1.984 – mil novecientos ochenta y cuatro; 2.025 – dos mil veinticinco

primera – Isabel; segunda – Elena; tercera – María

p. 23 (a) el diez de enero (b) el dieciséis de marzo (c) el veintidós de junio (d) el
primero de octubre (e) el quince de noviembre

p. 25 (a) a la una y cuarto (b) a las dos y media (c) a las tres menos cuarto (d) a las
cuatro en punto (e) a las cinco menos cuarto (f) a las trece cero cinco (g) a las catorce
veinticinco (h) a las dieciséis cincuenta y cinco (i) a las veintidós cuarenta y seis (j) a las
veintitrés cincuenta y nueve

p. 30 (a) detrás de la tapia (b) debajo de la mesa (c) delante del cine (d) entre sus
dueños

p. 32 (*suggested answers:*) (1) ¿Cuánto dinero tienes? (2) ¿Quién es Usted? (3) ¿Qué
coche tienes? (4) ¿Dónde está la bicicleta? (5) ¿Cómo estás?

p. 34 (1) este libro, estos libros; esta casa, estas casas; este coche, estos coches; esta
familia; este restaurante
(2) mi libro, mis libros; mi casa, mis casas; mi coche; mi familia; mi restaurante
(3) nuestro libro, nuestros libros; nuestra casa, nuestras casas; nuestro coche; nuestra
familia; nuestro restaurante

p. 47 (a) le gusta el vino (b) le gusta el queso (c) no le gustan los gatos (d) no le gustan
las arañas

p. 52 el pañal, el sonajero; el biberón; el chupete; el babero: ¡el bebé!

p. 57 (a) lleva botas de goma, pantalón, chaqueta y gorra (b) lleva zapatos de tacón,
falda, cinturón y camiseta (c) lleva un bikini (d) lleva un pantalón de baño

p. 59 (a) un suéter (b) una falda (c) unos guantes (d) una camisa (e) unos calcetines (f)
una camiseta (g) unos pantalones (h) un pijama

p. 61 (a) un anillo (b) unos pendientes (c) un collar (d) un perfume (e) un vaporizador

p. 68 (a) dos copas de vino blanco y una copa de vino tinto (b) tres cervezas (c) un café
solo y dos cafés con leche

p. 76 (*clockwise from top left*) dormitorio; dormitorio; cocina; salón-comedor; aseo;
cuarto de baño

p. 78 (a) un sillón nuevo para la sala de estar (b) un espejo nuevo para el dormitorio

(*c*) una lámpara nueva para el comedor (*d*) un lavabo nuevo para el cuarto de baño
(*e*) una cocina de gas nueva para la cocina (*f*) una cama nueva para el dormitorio
(*g*) una cómoda nueva para el dormitorio (*h*) una lavadora nueva para la cocina

p. 97   (*a*) el ordenador (*b*) el escritorio/ la mesa (*c*) la silla giratoria (*d*) la lámpara de mesa (*e*) el teléfono (*f*) la carta (*g*) la calculadora (*h*) la pluma

p. 99   (*a*) tengo una cita a las 10.00 con el dentista (*b*) tengo un compromiso para jugar al golf (*c*) tengo demasiado trabajo (*d*) No puedo, tengo un compromiso para comer

p. 123		
banój –	mi jabón
epien –	mi piene
posjean –	mi esponja
znispa –	mis pinzas
dsareco –	mi secador

p. 156   (*a*) en autobús (*b*) en taxi (*c*) en avión (*d*) en tranvía (*e*) en motocicleta (*f*) en bicicleta (*g*) en tren (*h*) en barco

p. 167   (*a*) la marisma; (*b*) el árbol de hoja caduca; (*c*) el árbol conífero; (*d*) la montaña; (*e*) el castillo; (*f*) el lago; (*g*) la iglesia